Bolt from the Blue
WILD PEREGRINES ON THE HUNT

Dedication

*In celebration of
the return of the peregrine.
Dedicated to those who
made it happen.*

Bolt from the Blue
WILD PEREGRINES ON THE HUNT

Dick Dekker

hancock

house

ISBN 0-88839-434-9

Cataloging in Publication Data
Dekker, Dick, 1933-
   Bolt from the blue

   ISBN 0-88839-434-9
   1. Peregrine falcon. I. Court, Gordon Stuart, 1959- II. Title.
QL696.F34D35 1999   598.9'6   C98-910502-4

We acknowledge the financial support of the Government of Canada through the
Book Publishing Industry Development Program for our publishing activities.

Editing and line drawings by the author.
Production: Ingrid Luters and Nancy Miller
Cover photograph: Dr. Gordon Court
All photos by Dr. Gordon Court unless indicated otherwise.

Published simultaneously in Canada and the United States by

HANCOCK HOUSE PUBLISHERS LTD.
19313 Zero Avenue, Surrey, B.C. V4P 1M7
(604) 538-1114 Fax (604) 538-2262

HANCOCK HOUSE PUBLISHERS
1431 Harrison Avenue, Blaine, WA 98230
(604) 538-1114 Fax (604) 538-2262
Web Site: www.hancockhouse.com *email:* sales@hancockhouse.com

Contents

Acknowledgments

A small gesture of kindness sometimes goes a long way. Many years ago, the late Dr. Otto Höhn, a fellow member of the Edmonton Bird Club, upon hearing that I was interested in birds of prey, gave me a copy of Rudebeck's paper on hunting by raptorial birds. It opened a new world for me, that of the scientific literature. With a limited education and never having read a single research paper, I was amazed what one could do with direct field observation. Up to that point I had scrupulously entered all noteworthy sightings on the behavior of falcons and hawks in a detailed journal. I now saw a way of organizing this material into a paper acceptable to a professional journal. Dr. David Boag of the University of Alberta kindly reviewed my first effort and made helpful comments. My observations on peregrines at Beaverhills Lake, from 1969 to 1983, were encouraged and supervised by William Wishart, then director of research at the Alberta Fish and Wildlife Division, which reimbursed some of my expenses. To widen my perspective, I applied for a chance to observe the foraging habits of breeding peregrines in the Peace-Athabasca delta, which was arranged by Richard Fyfe of the Canadian Wildlife Service. In 1995, Dr. Wayne Nelson kindly invited me to accompany him on one of his ten-day breeding surveys of the peregrines of Langara in the Queen Charlotte Islands. It led to a subsequent period of fruitful observation on the hunting habits of these falcons, as described in chapter eight. While on Langara, lightkeepers Judy and Gorden Schweers provided wonderful hospitality. Edo and Elizabeth Nyland were generous hosts while I was watching peregrines on Vancouver Island.

As to this book, I would like to thank David Hancock who has been a peregrine aficionado for as long as I have. As publisher, he made it possible, for me as well as for other authors with falcons on their mind, to see personal experiences and ideas in print. Dr. Wayne Nelson provided relevant literature and made helpful comments on the first chapters of an earlier version of the manuscript. In addition to reviewing the text, Dr. Gordon Court contributed the foreword and most of the photographs, which greatly enhance this publication.

If my choice of words, a phrase here and there, seems reminiscent of the writings of J. A. Baker, it is entirely unintentional but hard to avoid. Although it is more than fifteen years ago that I last read his diary, its descriptive prose haunts me still. By and large I have found Baker's insights regarding the hunting habits of wintering British peregrines to hold true for some of my observations in Canada. Curiously, he never seemed to have come across falcons just after they had made their kill out of sight, which was a common experience for me. Nor did he describe any aggressive interactions with other raptors, a daily routine for peregrines here.

Last but not least, I am grateful to Irma and our son Richard who cheerfully put up with a frequently absent husband and father. To her everlasting credit, my dear spouse is quite unlike the lady mentioned in Shakespeare's Merry Wives of Windsor: "She laments, sire.... her husband goes this morning a-birding."

Sharply etched against the bright western light . . . ,
they fell like meteors, here one moment, gone the next.

Foreword

A field day with the ultimate watcher

I first met Dick Dekker more than twenty years ago in the 'wilds' of a south Edmonton parking lot surrounding the O. S. Longman laboratory building, then site of the first hack release of captive-raised peregrine falcons in Canada. As we both marveled at the sight of 'man-made' peregrines taking their maiden flights off an office building, Dick, in his humble manner, recounted details of the many hunts by wild peregrines that he had witnessed at Beaverhills Lake in central Alberta. I was impressed by the matter-of-fact way in which he described the details of these hunts. Some pursuits were spectacular, in others the falcon might be clumsy or lackadaisical, but Dick made no attempt to embellish his descriptions. Listening, I knew it was only a matter of time until I convinced him to take me out to one of his favorite observation posts to see these wild peregrines in action.

One fine spring day, I accompanied Dick to Beaverhills Lake. This huge prairie slough is an internationally renowned birding hotspot. But, to the uninitiated, hawk watching there was quite unlike any of the recreational birding I had come to appreciate. Watching for migrating peregrines with Dick seemed, at first, about as inspiring as watching paint dry. After a few hours in the field, it became very apparent to me that he is a man possessed of incredible patience—the Ultimate Watcher. Dick positioned his car about a quarter-mile from the lake (and consequently the same distance from most of the bird life in the area) and repetitively searched the sky and surrounding landscape with binoculars for hour upon hour. Under these conditions, I rapidly lost interest in scanning apparently empty skies, so it was not surprising that Dick saw the first peregrine of the day, an adult coursing low and fast down the shore. Although it was a relief to see any falcon after such a wait, in an instant it had stroked by us and was gone—not much of a reward for four hours of sitting.

At this point Dick made himself more comfortable by propping against a fence post and began scanning the sky once more with eight-power binoculars. After nearly half an hour, he announced he had a peregrine in view. Apparently, it was soaring several thousand feet high some distance to the south of us. As a fledgling graduate student, educated in the sciences, I had been trained to be skeptical. In fact, obnoxious incredulity was characteristic of my zoological colleagues in graduate school at the time and I also wore the mark well. As Dick announced that there was a 90 percent chance that the dot in the stratosphere that he was watching was a peregrine, I muttered to myself a very doubting: "Yeah...right." I searched the same sky, attempting to line up my ten-power binoculars with Dick's. Shortly, I picked up a large hawk soaring very high in the same area. Smugly I suggested that there was a buteo in Dick's field of view. He gently adjusted my sights by saying: "I can see the red-tail, the peregrine is at least a thousand feet higher." Back to scanning.

Despite my efforts, I could not pick up the soaring falcon. It was only Dick's enthusiasm and persistence to keep his glasses on the bird that convinced me he was watching anything at all. Without missing a beat, Dick soon began an excited narrative on the behavior of this dust speck. With his tempered Dutch accent, he proclaimed: "It's stoooping!...It's stoooping! There! A tremennnndous stoooop!" Knowing that I had no chance of picking up the bird now, he instructed: "Watch the lake! Watch the ducks!" Feeling like a very inept, novice birder, I followed his directions and quickly glassed the lake. In an instant the tranquil shore exploded into life. Ducks and shorebirds were up and headed in a thousand different directions. Only then did I detect what can truly be described as a "bolt from the blue." By the time I fixed my binoculars on this missile, it was skying back up like a rocket; in the parlance of falconers, it was "throwing up" with the momentum of the stoop. In a blink, I lost it from view.

I was somewhat dazed by the utterly spectacular nature of what I had just witnessed. The disappearance of the falcon made me wonder for a moment whether I had imagined the whole thing! I looked around to see what had become of Dick and found him fixing a spotting scope on a site about one quarter of a mile away. "It's an adult, very white in front, like the *tundrius* birds you study, maybe one of yours," he mused. Dick had found the falcon standing in the grass, even though the only visible portion of the bird was the head and neck. From its behavior—head bobbing up and down—it was apparent that it had made a kill. Soon, the peregrine was again on its way and I charged out over the muddy pasture to the kill site to complete the observation by identifying prey. On a grassy hummock, I found the scattered remains of a sandpiper.

In the confusion of this event, neither Dick nor I had seen the terminus of the hunt—the actual strike. The fact that we had both missed the critical moment made me feel a bit better about staring blankly at the sky earlier. As for Dick, this demonstration of his ability to find and watch hunting falcons remains the most impressive example of natural history observation that I have yet witnessed in my twenty years as a professional biologist. Remarkably, Dick Dekker has honed this skill to such a degree that observing hunting falcons is almost routine. Unlike most people in the modern western world, he has been able to dedicate the time and effort needed to indulge this avocation. He has been witness to more than 2,000 hunts by wild peregrines! Such experience is unique. Scientists who study these falcons, on or off the breeding grounds, can rarely afford the time (and many may lack the will) to look at the foraging behavior of peregrines in anything more than a cursory manner. Even the finest practitioners of the sport of falconry, who design or contrive the hunting opportunities for some superb captive falcons, rarely will have amassed the variety of experiences recorded by Dick Dekker.

Fortunately for us all, Dick is also blessed with the ability to recount his observations in the printed word. He has published his findings in peer-reviewed ornithological journals as well as in a popular forum, in the spirit of great peregrine watchers like J. A. Baker. Bolt from the Blue summarizes a lifetime of peregrine watching in an informative, popular style. Delightfully, what is written contains the same accurate and honest natural history observations that you will find in the research publications of the author.

In closing, I would remind the reader that the peregrine falcon is, without question, the most-studied raptorial bird in the world. Despite this attention, it is astounding just how much more we have to learn about this animal. In the pages that follow, Dick Dekker provides new insight on the foraging behavior of this species in a variety of habitats during breeding, migration and wintering stages of its annual cycle. I believe that it cannot be overstated that such insight has been obtained entirely from observations of free-ranging, wild falcons. In reading this volume, through Dekker's eyes, you, like me, will enjoy a privileged glimpse into the world of the hunting peregrine.

GORDON COURT, PH.D.
Edmonton, May 1998

Preface

The passionate eye

One leg slung over the saddle of my bicycle, I had stopped to look through my very first pair of binoculars, an ancient marine instrument made of heavy brass that I had just acquired through an ad in the local paper. On this bright winter day, the view of half a dozen mergansers, floating in an open lead of a partly frozen canal, was stunningly beautiful. Their regal crests and gorgeous colors were reflected in the water. Here in the Dutch lowlands, these divers were uncommon winter visitors, only migrating down from the North when extreme cold forced them out of their usual haunts. Suddenly, there was a great splash as another bird plunged down among them, falling quite vertically down from the sky. It was a smew, a small white and black diver, also a winter visitor from the North. Puzzled by the abruptness of its entry, instead of the typical gliding descent, I happened to look up and saw a large falcon sailing over the waterhole, her white chest gleaming in the winter sun. The thrill of the sighting almost made me fall off my bike, forcing me to let go of the falcon for a moment. When I found her again, she had turned away, her long wings flicking hurriedly until she vanished between the farms and windbreaks in the polder landscape on the other side of the canal.

It was not quite my very first peregrine. During the preceding fall, I had spotted one just as it alighted in the crown of a large oak. But I had been unable to get a good view, try as I might, scrutinizing the tangled branches through a long, brass telescope. Its unwieldy shape and very narrow field of view made it next to useless for watching birds. Yet, this archaic eye piece, borrowed from my dad, had opened up an entirely new world, one that was in sharp focus instead of fuzzy.

Some say that mankind's most revolutionary invention is the wheel. This may be a matter of opinion. I am inclined to nominate the field glass. Those who have less than perfect eye sight might well agree. As a kid, reading often by poor light on dark winter evenings, my view of the world was like an impressionist painting. At school, the teacher's handwriting on the blackboard was a gray, undecipherable scribble. Little did I know that other kids saw things through different eyes. In normal times, my sight would have been corrected, probably leading to ever-stronger glasses as my eyes grew lazy. But I was left alone and never tested. This was more than half a century ago.

A turning point arrived in my midteens when a scout leader allowed me a brief look through his binoculars. He had spotted a kestrel on a post. It was a revelation to be able to see the bird sharply outlined and in intimate detail: the narrow malar stripe, the brick-brown of its plumage. When the kestrel turned its head, the sun glinted in its eye. I felt as if I had been let in on a secret. I vividly remember that day, long ago, because I still feel the same thrill of suspense every time I watch a falcon on the lookout for prey.

Nowadays, people who hear that I see a lot more peregrines than most are quick to assume: "You must have good eyes!" Not so. But I stubbornly refuse to wear glasses and compensate by using the binoculars a lot. Like a falcon sitting on a post, continually turning its head and watching its surroundings, I scan the countryside far and near. This way I can pick up a distant peregrine that otherwise would have remained unseen.

Witness at the kill

Spotting a peregrine and watching it capture a prey are two very different things. And it is the latter I wanted most. The interest I take in falcons, my passionate obsession if you like, derives from a sublimated hunting instinct, a visceral urge to identify with the hunter, albeit vicariously, to share its mastery of the wind, its dominion over all below. There are few sights in nature that surpass the excitement of seeing a peregrine stoop from the clouds, striking its prey low over the ground. How rarely are such spectacles witnessed by humans. Yet, they may take place all around us, every day. To the falcon, hunting is a basic necessity, the only way it knows how to survive. For us, watching it at every opportunity, a few treasured moments at a time, is the only way to obtain a deep appreciation of the life of this accomplished creature.

My first observation of a hunting falcon dates back far into the past, to the time when I focused my newly acquired binoculars on the adult which had apparently just sent the smew head-over-heels into the waterhole. Hoping to find the falcon again and to see her actually in pursuit of her prey, I went back to the same spot several weekends in a row. One misty day she passed right overhead, a pigeon clutched in her feet. She flew to a tall power pylon across the road and alighted on a horizontal bar somewhere in the center. Soon, feathers began drifting down. Higher up in the same pylon, I discovered another peregrine, a smaller one. A few minutes later, he left, descending low and fast over a meadow. Then he slammed down. Oddly, after he landed he did not sit still but began to zigzag over the grass, wings flapping for balance as if he were riding an erratic toy. Presently, he came to a halt and his bobbing head seemed to indicate he was feeding. Due to the poor light I was greatly puzzled as to what exactly had taken place. Eager to investigate, I jumped across the water-filled ditch by the road and slogged to the far side of the meadow. His prey turned out to be a wigeon!

This was my very first kill and already I had learned that the peregrine, this fabled aerial hunter, does not always go by the book. Instead of striking his prey high in the sky and knocking it down, this adult tiercel had grabbed the duck on or just over the grass! The few bird books we had in those days did not prepare you for that. Nor did they inform you that falcons, instead of always perching on a high lookout, sometimes just sat on the ground. This was the way I located my next peregrine, and again the bird ended up doing something that seemed very odd. When it flew, instead of launching an exciting pursuit as I had hoped, it flushed a sparrowhawk from the edge of a ditch. The hawk was carrying a prey, a redwing thrush. He quickly dropped it, and the falcon picked it up. So much for the greatest hunter of the avian world!

These early observations, however, neither disappointed nor shocked me. On the contrary I found them highly intriguing and I desperately longed to learn more. As that lyrical British peregrine watcher J. A. Baker phrased it: "The eye becomes insatiable for hawks, it clicks towards them with ecstatic fury." So it is with me. The mind is swept clean like an empty canvas. Projected on the retina, the falcon is framed in a circle of intense light too bright to endure, and I ache to see it again and again.

When at last I experienced the classical hunt, a stoop at a pigeon right overhead, the pullout sounded like the crack of a whip. Missing her target, the peregrine chased the pigeon low over the heather. At the falcon's next shallow pass, the prey lost a puff of feathers but managed to fly on and reach a copse of trees, where I later found it stone-dead, a large bloody wound in its chest. This hunt, in which the falcon had hit her prey in the air, may seem very typical for a peregrine. Yet, I now know that this early kill was unique in its own way, perhaps more so than a tiercel grabbing a duck on the ground or robbing a sparrowhawk.

A new start

My first chance to observe peregrines at the nest came after I had moved to the province of Alberta in western Canada. In those days it was still not difficult to locate half a dozen eyries on any river flowing east from the Rocky Mountains. I centered my springtime searches on a twenty-mile (32 km) stretch of the Red Deer River. Here, there were at least four breeding pairs of peregrines and about the same number of prairie falcons. Later, I narrowed my investigations to what I came to call the "Valley of the Falcons." No more than four miles (6.4 km) long, it contained two peregrine cliffs and two or three traditional prairie falcon eyries. Interestingly, there seemed little strife between the two species, at least after the breeding season had started and during the relatively short period when I visited the valley.

In the sixties, when news of the disastrous side effects of pesticides exploded like a bomb in the western world, nature lovers everywhere were deeply concerned, but perhaps none more so than falcon aficionados. I do not think that young people today realize the sense of doom we felt when told that our favorite bird would cease to exist on this planet and that other falcons and hawks were next. The Valley of the Falcons was not spared. In 1967, the last pair of peregrines on the Red Deer River failed to fledge young. However, the prairie falcons seemed the big winners. Their population was expanding and to this day they are thriving.

Looked at objectively, the peregrine's local demise might have had a number of other causes besides the slow poisoning of its prey base and eggs by toxic chemical residues. During the fifties and sixties major changes in agricultural practices were sweeping the plains. Vast monocultures left no room for songbirds. Feral pigeons lost out when old-time wooden granaries were destroyed. The few gray partridges and ducks that managed to nest in narrow, sprayed ditches ran an increased risk of coyote and fox predation. The numbers of wetland birds were greatly reduced after sloughs and marshes had been drained or dried up. The fact that the bird-hunting peregrine disappeared whereas the prairie falcon thrived, might have been a consequence of changes in habitat and prey base. Prairie falcons, which are well-adapted to arid conditions, eat mainly ground squirrels during spring and early summer. Moreover, it was a fact that the local peregrines had suffered much from direct human interference. During the critical years in Alberta, many if not all of the last eyries were robbed of young by professional animal dealers.

In retrospect, I regret that the last wild peregrines of this river had not been taken into captivity as seed stock for captive breeding. This would have preserved the genes of the local *anatum* dynasty. However, during the midsixties such novel ideas had not yet proven themselves, and I was one of those who preferred to leave the last of the peregrines alone and enforce their protection in the fervent hope they would survive the bad years and make a comeback on their own once environmental pollution had eased. This did not happen. Even after three decades, when many other regional peregrine populations had rebounded, the only occupants of the cliffs in the Valley of the Falcons were prairie falcons.

In 1993, federal and provincial wildlife agencies in Canada, backed by private sponsors, made a major commitment for a mass release of juvenile peregrines in central and southern Alberta. More than 200 young, produced by Phil and Helen Trefry in the breeding facility of the Canadian Wildlife Service at Wainwright, were hacked out over three summers. Several of the release locations were down-stream from the Valley of the Falcons. To everyone's delight this her-culean, last-chance effort caught on, and by 1997 the first pair of captive-raised peregrines, after safely returning from their second migration, nested and fledged young on a natural site of their own choice. Amazingly, as described in chapter four, they picked exactly the same cliff where I had observed the last pair thirty years earlier! As of this writing, the number of peregrines breeding on the Red Deer has increased to three or four pairs. Their future will be watched with a great deal of interest and satisfaction by those who were involved in this marvelous project! Incidentally, the recoloniz-ing peregrines did not seem to have much trouble with the prairie falcons, outflying and outperforming the latter in aerial battles that left little doubt as to the victor.

If I have one regret, after spending so much time watching pere-grines on the Red Deer, it is that I never saw any hunting activity there. By and large, the river was too narrow. The falcons appeared to do all of their foraging well away from the valley. During fair weather, they soared and sailed over the plains, disappearing from view for as long as four hours, or returning with a blackbird or other small prey a few minutes later.

Falcons far and near

My chances of seeing peregrines in action greatly improved after moving to the city of Edmonton. The open shores of nearby Beaverhills Lake proved ideal for observing migrants. These falcons hunted mainly ducks and sandpipers, as described in chapters five, six and seven. Each spring from 1969 to 1983, I took a four-week leave of absence from my work as a free-lance graphic designer to conduct a singular survey. In addition to recording migration dates and adult-immature ratios, I noted all hunting activity and collect-ed prey remains for toxic chemical analysis. The results were assem-bled into annual reports and published in the research papers listed in the reference pages. For an inland location, I saw a lot of pere-grines. The seasonal average for the last ten years (after I had learned how to look) was 75; the most ever was 163 in 1977. Spring migration occurred from 15 April to the end of May, even into the first days of June. The number of sightings, or mean, per observer/hour was 0.32, which compares quite well with coastal migration studies.

For most of the season, I stayed in the field for several days at a stretch, sleeping in an abandoned farmhouse with hordes of mice running over my bed and a great-horned owl hooting on the chimney. Despite the pastoral setting, the bellowing of cattle and barking of dogs were often hard to take. One full moon night, I packed up and parked my trusty Volvo wagon by the lake to be serenaded by frogs, snipe and bitterns. It proved to be a good move. It is amazing what you can see while having breakfast on the tail gate or sitting quietly against a fence post. More than once, a tiercel landed on a post nearby. When he bowed and ee-chupped, I never knew whether he was addressing me or another unseen falcon. Sometimes he cackled as if upset or indignant about my presence, before leaving in apparent haste.

There were also numerous intimate moments with other wildlife, common and rare, and I kept track of the timing of migrations of a number of species, including shorebirds. There was much to see and enjoy. Maximizing my time afield, I begrudged even the one day a week I was expected to come home. Migration is not a steady process. Driven by the vagaries of weather, a wave of birds might come in by late afternoon. Next morning all could be gone. Having learned to recognize conditions that herald a good day, I was often loath to leave before dark. Nowadays, I still go to the lake, quite often in fact, but I rarely stay longer than four or five hours. As a consequence, my tally of peregrines is a fraction of what it used to be. Some springs I count less than a dozen and see very little hunting action. Once the passion is spent, our eyes look inward and fail to note the magic that surrounds us in the natural world.

My obsession was rekindled by a change of scene. Since 1980, to escape Alberta's subarctic winter, I go for a few weeks to western British Columbia, as detailed in chapters nine, ten and eleven. The rain-shrouded coast of the north Pacific may not be the ideal resort to most people, but for me it was second heaven. A lowland peasant by origin, I thrive in the peregrine's preferred winter habitat, the muddy interface of land and water. Rubber boots are my favorite footwear. Each new morning on the coast or in a waterlogged field held the promise of discovery and adventure. No two days were the same. Some were frustrating and unproductive if I found myself repeatedly in the wrong place at the wrong time. On other days I was witness to the kill. The key to success was to persevere, to turn inward and sink into the landscape, contemplating the drift of clouds and the slow change of light. The passionate eye had to be tempered with patience.

All incidents and observations described in the following chapters are exactly as they happened. When relevant, the activities of the observer will be mentioned as well for they are part of the story. I will try to convey to the reader the essence of the hunting life, the bone-chilling boredom of sitting hunched up for hours in wind and rain, and the sudden exhilaration of watching a falcon outwit and outperform its prey, high in the sky or low over the ground.

Chapter 1

BULLET HAWK

One languid May evening, after a long walk over the open grasslands flanking Beaverhills Lake, I was sitting quietly by a dugout pond when my eyes focused on a pair of gadwall ducks approaching over the pasture. Suddenly, overhead, there was an explosive swoosh. Streaking down from the sky, a peregrine just missed the ducks, which splashed into the water. In a roar of wings, the falcon shot back up and left at once, beating hurriedly, glancing back over its shoulder at me.

Impressed by the violence of this close-up moment, it struck me that the old colloquial name for this bird was bullet hawk. It seemed right on the mark. Its Latin scientific name *Falco peregrinus* means wanderer, denoting its migratory habits. So does its name in various other languages: *Wanderfalk* (German), *pilgrimsfalk* (Swedish) and *faucon pèlerin* (French). In Holland, which was once renowned for the skill of its falconers, the peregrine is called *slechtvalk*. The word *slecht* means common in archaic Dutch. Formerly, this deadly and spectacular raptor, this bolt from the blue, used to be common indeed, wherever there were birds to be preyed upon and enough open space to launch a long-range attack. Before the British name peregrine came into general use, the common American label was duck hawk. It too was quite to the point, for this falcon is fond of ducks and capable of knocking one out of the sky as if it were hit by a bullet.

World wanderer

The most cosmopolitan of birds, the peregrine is an extremely successful species that has colonized all continents except Antarctica and some oceanic islands including New Zealand. Oddly, it is absent from Iceland, perhaps because of competition from the larger and more powerful gyrfalcon that makes its home in the barrenlands. The peregrine does not thrive in arid regions. In deserts and steppes of Asia, Africa and eastern Europe, it is replaced by lanners and sakers, close relatives of the North American prairie falcon. These dry-country falcons, including the gyr of the northern tundra, take a wide range of prey including rodents, whereas the peregrine is almost exclusively a bird specialist. Only in the Arctic, where avian prey can be few and far between, do some peregrines utilize lemmings and ground squirrels as an important portion of their diet. This is one of the surprising discoveries of Canadian researchers such as Gordon Court.

Peregrines belong to the genus *Falco* which, worldwide, includes some twenty-five closely related species varying from the tiny kestrel weighing less than seven ounces (200 g) to the seventy-ounce (2,000 g) gyrfalcon. *Falco peregrinus* has the widest distribution of all. Scientists recognize some twenty-two geographic races or subspecies of peregrines, which show the same basic physical characteristics and habits but differ in size and color. Generally, birds that live in colder climates are larger than those in warmer regions. The largest races have a wingspan of just more than three feet (1 m) and weigh 28–50 ounces (800–1,400 g), almost twice as much as the smallest races that range from 16–28 ounces (450–800 g). Tropical representatives are brightly colored, while the palest birds are found in northern Europe and Siberia.

Three races of peregrines have been recognized in North America. The most widespread is *F. p. anatum* (freely translated: the one that kills ducks), which is among the largest and most beautiful of peregrines in the world. Typical individuals feature a pinkish or salmon-colored glow on the chest. The *anatum* used to nest across the continent and still survives in western regions from California to Canada. The northwest Pacific Coast and the Aleutian Islands are inhabited by the Peale's peregrine (*F. p. pealei*), which is considered the heaviest and darkest of all. Surprisingly, the race that breeds farthest north, the tundra peregrine (*F. p. tundrius*), is the smallest. It forms an exception to Bergmann's Rule, which states that of any warm-blooded species of animal the larger races are found in colder latitudes. The increased size reduces the surface to volume ratio and therefore limits heat loss, an important adaptation to the climate. The explanation for the tundra falcon's small size may be found in the fact that this race actually spends more time on migration and on its wintering grounds, where it enjoys the summer of the southern hemisphere, than on Arctic breeding territory. Its wings are also relatively longer and narrower than in peregrines that spend the year in more temperate regions and occupy the best habitats closest to home. To find vacant winter range, Arctic migrants are forced to cover immense distances twice yearly, leapfrogging over the occupied territories of their relatives.

Based on the proportions and plumage of falcons I see migrating over central Alberta, a case could be made for recognizing a fourth geographic race that is perhaps typical of the boreal forest regions of the continent. It is quite slender, of medium size and darker than *tundrius*, especially the immatures. Some adult females are dorsally blackish brown or slate brown rather than gray or bluish. In the field and in the hand, racial differences are obscured by individual variation. However, the fact that some regional populations are consistently larger and heavier than others is undeniable if you have seen the massive females of the northwest Pacific Coast, or if you had the opportunity, long ago, of observing the true, continental *anatum*.

Mark of distinction

With its boldly marked head and bright, yellow-rimmed eyes the adult peregrine is a strikingly handsome bird. The hallmark of the species is a prominent malar stripe or moustache. Its function, if there is one, is obscure. The black color under the eye may reduce glare. Or perhaps the contrasting facial mask is designed to startle prey at close range and flush it out of cover. The shape of the malar bar varies. In some birds it is so wide as to merge with the nape, practically forming a black hood. In others, particularly in the tundra peregrine, the stripe is narrower. The color of the bare skin or cere around the eyes and at the base of the bill also varies, from bright to pale yellow or whitish, possibly depending on the bird's diet. To the expert, the heads of peregrines are as individual as the faces of people. At nest sites in the Queen Charlotte Islands, researcher Wayne Nelson makes detailed drawings and photographs of a pair's characteristics that hold true from year to year and help him recognize these individuals later.

Apart from facial detail, there is a host of other obvious and subtle differences that distinguish one bird from the other. No doubt, mated pairs can recognize each other from great distances by outline and behavior. In flight, some falcons look more compact or slimmer than others. They differ in color as well. Dorsally—on the upper side of wings, back and tail—adults can be bluish gray, slate gray or even blackish brown. In some birds the dorsal color is plain, in others it is variegated: lightest on the pearl gray rump and darkening to black on the tail and primaries. Up close, the markings on the belly and flanks of adults vary from heavy barring to light spotting.

Young birds show a similar range of variation. Before they begin to molt into adult plumage, which starts in the second summer, their under- or ventral side is streaked, boldly in some, lightly in others. Dorsally they are dark brown, but tundra birds can be a sandy brown that makes them look more like a prairie falcon than a typical peregrine. Some northern immatures even lack the dark crown and are startlingly blond-headed. These birds look very different from the usual illustrations of the species in handbooks and field guides, which often fail to explain the extensive plumage variation. In the field, you will rarely see quite that same detailed and colorful image. The wild bird may be no more than a speck in the sky or a monochrome silhouette in a wide landscape.

The odd couple

When you observe a pair of falcons together, soaring over their nesting territory, it is usually obvious that they differ in size. In most animal species, the male is bigger than the female, but not in raptors. This curious phenomenon is termed reversed sexual dimorphism.

Simply stated, it means that females are larger than males. Generally, the size difference between the sexes is greatest in bird hunters, and least in raptors that subsist mainly on mammals or insects. It is nonexistent in vultures, where males may be even bigger than females.

In peregrines, the male or tiercel is about 30 percent smaller and lighter than his partner. This difference widens between the races; a male of the smallest race and a female of the largest race would make an odd couple indeed. If you see an exceptionally small tiercel darting like an excited dwarf around a big falcon, it can be hard to believe that both belong to the same species! On the other hand, within the same race, male and female can be quite similar in size since there is a fair amount of individual variation. If a nesting pair happens to consist of a smallish female and a robust tiercel, it can be difficult to tell them apart. There is also gradual overlap between geographic populations. The upshot is that no two peregrines are exactly alike, which makes it often tricky or even impossible to classify them as to race or sex, particularly in the field.

Why the female is generally larger than her mate continues to be the subject of scientific debate. Half a dozen theories have been postulated and scores of papers have been written about this puzzling phenomenon. A prominent hypothesis is that the difference in size allows the pair to take advantage of a wider range of prey. This theory is discounted by some authors, who point out that both sexes often catch the same prey species. This may indeed be the case, particularly in countries such as Britain where feral pigeons are the peregrine's mainstay. Similarly, on the Queen Charlotte Islands both sexes capture the same kinds of small sea birds, at least for part of the year. However, during winter and migration, on the coast as well as on the interior prairies, the diet of the two sexes can be significantly different, reducing competition between them. While the big females hunt primarily ducks, the males tend to specialize on sandpipers or passerines. Typically, the female tolerates males on her winter territory, but she will immediately launch a fierce offense if a female comes into view. Very recently, in 1998, when I began to observe a pair of falcons nesting at Wabamun Lake in central Alberta, I was struck by the obvious difference in the kinds of prey taken by the two sexes. While the male hunted nearly exclusively small passerines and shorebirds, the female took mainly gulls and ducks.

An alternative theory explaining reversed sexual dimorphism suggests that males are better providers, since they require less food for themselves and are more successful at capturing small prey of a weight that can be carried to the nest. Adult males frequently manage to catch 20 or 30 percent of the shorebirds and passerines they chase, whereas the overall average of the species is usually around 10 percent. Even though the male is quite capable of killing ducks, he cannot carry a wigeon or pintail. Nor can he defend his prey against piracy attempts by harriers and buteos. On the other hand, the female is quite capable of warding off most other hawks. For her, eating a substantial meal, such as a duck, is particularly important just prior to egg-laying time. A breeding female puts on 10 to 20 percent more body weight. Lethargic and slow, she becomes dependent upon the smaller and more agile male, which will continue to provide for her until well after the eggs have hatched and the chicks are about three weeks old.

Another and complementary theory is that bigger females are better breeders. Because of their large body size, they can produce bigger eggs, have more body heat for incubation and are better at defending the nest against rivals and potential nest robbers. All of the above reasons appear to make sense and may operate at the same time. Nature usually has more than one arrow on its bow. Over aeons of time, through the process of natural selection, each sex of the peregrine appears to have reached its optimal size. The male increased his foraging efficiency by becoming as small as he can afford to be, while the female maximized her bulk and her brood's chances for survival in the unconscious knowledge that a bigger mother is a better mother.

In addition to the variation in size and plumage, individual peregrines also differ in behavior, temperament, prey preference and hunting skills. Each falcon is a personality in its own right. By watching patiently over many years, we can learn to recognize individual characteristics and get to know a falcon as well as it is possible to understand a creature that is so unlike us. Belonging to another realm, supreme at the top of the trophic pyramid, the peregrine is an eminently successful species that has maintained itself infinitely longer than *Homo sapiens*, the plodding biped that evolved from primeval cave-crawling ancestors relatively recently in geological time.

Super athlete

To the perceptive observer, a close look at the peregrine suffices to place it in an exclusive category all its own. As it rushes by in typically hurried flight, the supple wingbeats betray the superior athlete. If you happen to find a pinion feather, perhaps below a nest or a favorite perch, it feels surprisingly firm and stiff. A bent tip snaps back smartly. In peregrines, the second primary from the tip is longest, making the wing sharply pointed, more so than in other hawks. When fully extended, the falcon's wings are quite straight without much of a bend at the carpal joint. Based on the ratio of body weight to wing surface, the peregrine is said to have a high wingloading. Its heavy, muscular body combined with narrow wings favors speed, in contrast to birds with a light wingloading, such as buteos or eagles, which have relatively large wings that allow slow, sailing flight. The peregrine certainly can soar with the best of them and does so routinely. Like the long-winged gulls, falcons love the wind and even try to soar during rain. However, their speed when circling high in the sky is always faster than other hawks.

What makes watching this bird such a thrill is the fact that it can vary its pace and accelerate at any moment. Flying leisurely, flapping and sailing, it may suddenly decide to launch an attack and increase its beat dramatically to a furious crescendo. In the terminal stoop, it folds its wings close to the tail and becomes a streak upon the eye. The next instant it shoots back up like a rocket, curving over and down again for a second pass at the dodging target, or to resume its soaring pitch.

The top speed of peregrines has been variously calculated and measured as 100–235 miles (160–380 km) per hour. This occurs only during brief moments when the falcon plummets earthward, assisted by gravity. In level flapping flight its speed may be no more than sixty miles per hour (100 km), about the same as a cheetah running flat out. In fact, unless it has a headstart or superior height, a peregrine may have trouble overtaking its favorite prey, such as pigeons or ducks. To capture them, it often uses strategy and takes advantage of the target's mistakes. A matter of life and death, the contest between prey and predator is exciting to watch whether we identify with the hunter or the hunted. Although the outcome of their interaction is direct and final, the struggle is subtle and ever fascinating, no matter how often we have observed the ancient drama unfold.

The peerless eye

Sitting on a fence post, some distance away, the peregrine's silhouette looks quite different from other raptors in its size range. It lacks the bulkiness of the buteo, the loose feathering of the harrier and the tense stance of the accipiter. The falcon sits erect yet relaxed, looking broad-shouldered and lean, its long wings neatly crossed over the tapering tail. The head is rounded, the neck short. Close-up, the large eyes, dark and shiny, are its most striking feature. They lack the hard and hostile glare of the light-colored eyes of other raptors. By comparison, the peregrine's gaze is almost magnanimous, docile, free of menace.

The quality of the peregrine's eye, how well and what it sees, is another subject of speculation and research. If we had eyes of that caliber compared to body size, they would weigh about four pounds (1.8 kg) a piece. The peregrine has a wide angle of view. Anyone who has tried to walk up to a perched bird very soon discovers that little escapes its attention. Its head is never still, the brilliant eyes scanning horizon and sky, far and near. Yet, in the next moment they can focus on a target a mile away with uncanny resolution. Experts claim that a peregrine's vision is about eight times as acute as ours. This may well underestimate the falcon's real ability. For many years, I used high-quality binoculars with a magnification of eight. More than once have I seen falcons launch hunts at high-flying targets, such as a flock of ducks, which I picked up in the glasses well after the falcons had taken off from their perch. Seeing them start after a small passerine at astonishing distances was eloquent proof that peregrines had better eyes than mine assisted with an eight-power Zeiss.

Chapter 2

The Superlative Hunter

Riding the wind, high over the crest of a hill, the peregrine watches a pair of ducks fly up from a pond far below. Unaware of their peril, they leave the reedy shore and cross an open field. With a burst of wingbeats, the falcon gains speed, overtakes its target and stoops. Struck in midair, the drake cartwheels and bounces onto the stubble, dead or mortally wounded.

This is the way the peregrine's legendary prowess as a hunter is often described. Such spectacular strikes do indeed occur. However, they happen far less often than is generally believed. In well over 100 successful hunts whereby I could clearly see the moment of impact, the falcon simply grabbed the prey in its feet and brought it down to the ground or carried it to a perch. By comparison, I saw very few aerial hits, each of them a singular event. A teal, attacked head-on and from below, fluttered to the ground as if its wing had been broken. In two other memorable hunts, a pigeon and a small grebe were overtaken in level pursuit and struck, as evidenced by a burst of feathers, yet they flew on. Just as the falcon closed in for the second try, the grebe fell into bushes. The pigeon managed to reach a copse of trees but died from a large wound in its breast.

Once, while I sat by the lake, a peregrine stooped at a flock of sandpipers flushing from the shore right in front of me. One of the peeps ended up floating belly-up in the shallows, to be retrieved by the falcon. Such hits may be impossible to verify if peregrines attack small birds at some distance from the observer. A common phenomenon that makes the correct interpretation of distant hunts even more tricky is the fact that shorebirds and ducks routinely dodge raptors by plunging down. This happens in the very last split-second, which makes it look as if the bird was hit. Instead, it dove into water or sought safety in vegetation. After watching peregrines hunt at every opportunity over five decades, I thought I had seen all possible hunting methods until I began detailed observations in the Queen Charlotte Islands and on the mainland coast of British Columbia. There, I saw falcons smack sea birds floating on the water. Other peregrines, instead of just grabbing a small sandpiper, insisted on hitting it in the air, in the water or on the ground.

In contrast to my experience with wild falcons, knockdowns and aerial strikes are commonly reported by falconers who fly their peregrines at ducks and grouse. Circling overhead, the trained falcon waits for its keeper to flush the quarry. Reacting compulsively to the stimulus of prey rising below it, the falcon stoops at once, often at a very steep angle, and hits the mallard or partridge a stunning blow. However, in the wild, birds rarely flush directly below a peregrine. Experienced and deadly serious, most falcons launch long-range attacks, seize their prey in the air and carry it to a suitable feeding site. Smacking birds and allowing them to drop does not make sense if the falcon is hunting over reeds or trees, since the prey might not be retrievable. Nevertheless, it appears that knockdowns are performed by certain individuals more than by others. And if enraged, all peregrines attempt to strike their enemies, be they large birds, mammals and even humans, if they are perceived as a threat to eggs and young.

"Noble" killer

How the aerial knockout is actually delivered has been a subject for speculation over many years until the video camera provided some clear evidence. Close footage shows that the strike can be executed either with an open foot or a closed one. In the latter case, the front toes are folded out of the way and the protruding rear talon does all the damage. The leg or tarsus is short and sturdy, able to withstand sudden impact. The big feet of a falcon may not be ideal for getting about (seeing one walk is actually quite comical) but they are well designed for grabbing and holding on. The toes are long and flexible. They spread like a web and are armed with sharp talons. The rear claw is biggest. It can deliver a cut that slashes deep into living flesh. However, an aerial hit may simply be the result of a glancing and slightly off-center attempt at seizing that prey.

The usual instrument for killing is not the foot but the bill. Short and very powerful, the falcon's beak is especially designed for dispatching prey. On either side, the upper mandible features a triangular protrusion or tooth that fits in the notched lower mandible. Grasping the victim's neck and inserting its beak between the vertebrae, the peregrine severs the spinal cord with a twist and a tug, ending life relatively quickly. If the prey is a sandpiper, small passerine or pigeon, it may even be decapitated with one bite. By contrast, other bird-hunting raptors, such as the accipiters, do not have notched mandibles and kill with their claws. Standing on their catch, they knead it spasmodically, long nails piercing vital organs. If the bird or mammal is too large to be dispatched by their grasp, the hawk may begin eating before the prey has expired.

As a rule, the peregrine always kills its victim before feeding, a habit which we perceive as merciful, worthy of this "noble" predator. Small birds may be killed in flight. Bringing its feet forward, the falcon bends down to bite the prey. Usually, the *coup-de-grace* is administered after landing. Its grip on the prey appears to be quite light (or perhaps its feet are just too big to hold small birds) since sandpipers and passerines occasionally escape after the falcon has landed.

Hunting success

The question of how good peregrines are at their craft has been discussed at length in the scientific literature ever since the Swedish ornithologist Gustav Rudebeck published his 1950 paper, which was then rather controversial. He reported a hunting success rate of 7.3 percent in 250 observations of falcons attacking prey. At that time, many raptor authorities believed that this figure was far too low for a superlative predator like the peregrine. They seemed to be proven right when other observers recorded much higher rates of 25 to 35 percent during observations at peregrine nest sites in Britain, North Africa and Quebec. Why the great difference? Was it perhaps true, as the critics claimed, that the Swedish falcons, which were on migration, were not hunting seriously? Could they just have been fooling around?

It seems logical that migrants, unless they are very hungry, probably hunt with less determination than breeding peregrines, which need to forage for their brood. Moreover, nesting falcons are familiar with local opportunities and wait on strategic points for the right moment to attack vulnerable prey, often land birds flying over lakes and oceans. It is to be expected that these experienced adults have a higher success rate than migrating falcons, which feed along the way at their leisure and rather opportunistically in unfamiliar terrain. Moreover, the Swedish data, obtained during fall, included many immatures, which have less expertise as hunters than adults.

The validity of Rudebeck's low rate was underscored by my long-term observations on migrating peregrines at Beaverhills Lake in Alberta. I calculated a success rate of 7.7 percent, nearly equivalent to the Swedish figure, in well over 1,000 hunts. In this very large sample, obtained during spring, immatures had a success rate of about 7 percent whereas adults achieved close to 10 percent. I found a fairly similar value of 9.3 in 302 shorebird hunts by falcons wintering on the Pacific Coast. In comparison, territorial adults achieved respectively 20.9 and 21.9 percent success in hunting sea birds and ducks on Langara and Vancouver Island (see table in the back). Just recently, in 1997, I have begun observations at a nest site in central Alberta. As described in chapter fourteen, the success rate of this pair was in the same order of magnitude as the figures quoted above for territorial birds.

The growing literature on peregrines includes numerous other studies of hunting success although sample data may be rather small. Moreover, in evaluating them we need to know how the term "hunt" was defined. In the above cited calculations by Rudebeck and myself, a hunt means a completed attack directed at a single prey or a flock of prey of which the outcome was known. A hunt may include one or more passes at that same prey. However, if the falcon turns away and attacks another target, it begins a second hunt. Instead of following this simple rule, other observers use the term "hunting flight" which can include any number of attacks on different targets and may thus lead to a relatively higher success rate.

Attempts to express the interaction of peregrines and their prey in a mere cipher always fall short of the reality and excitement of a falcon in hot pursuit of its prey. However, at the very least the figures indicate that the large majority of prey manages to escape. Why some do and others do not is an intriguing question that touches on the falcon's selective effect. What makes it choose one prey over the other? Why does it persist in some pursuits and give up soon in others? Some people believe that a good falcon, given a fair chance, can catch any prey. This may be so. Fact is that it does not, because the prey has a mind of its own. The peregrine survives and prospers by virtue of its superior abilities as well as by taking advantage of the mistakes and weaknesses of its prey. The relationship between the two is intertwined and subject to an infinite set of variables, some of which are beyond our scope as observers. The fact that no two hunts are the same is exactly what makes watching peregrines so interesting, and it gets more fascinating the more we see.

Choice of prey

One May evening, I spotted an immature female peregrine perched on a fence post near Beaverhills Lake. She probably had just arrived after a long day of migratory flight and I assumed that she was hungry. Hoping to see her hunt, I sat down and waited. Soon she took off low for the reedy shore, where she made a quick turn and landed. Through the binoculars I could just make her out, screened by grass. Presently, her bobbing head movements indicated that she was feeding. It took only a few minutes. After she had finished and returned to a post, I searched for and found the remains of her meal: little more than a few feathers but enough to identify the prey as a least sandpiper. Surprised that this large female falcon had taken such a tiny bird, I continued watching. Evidently, the peep had only served as an appetizer. For, half an hour later, the falcon took off again. This time, she met a pair of gadwall ducks flying low over the pasture. Swooping up at them, she seized the drake, a prey that was roughly twenty times as heavy as the sandpiper.

Although peregrines can capture birds of a wide size range, they are limited to species that frequent open country. The bushes and reed beds may be alive with warblers and rails, but they are safe from the falcon as long as they stay in cover. "You are what you eat" is an adage that is usually applied to human nutrition and health. It is equally valid for the peregrine, the supreme aerial predator. It can only survive in environments that support enough birds it can catch and that make hunting them economical in terms of energy expended and gained.

Peregrines may become even more specialized during the breeding season when they depend largely on a few species. The ideal prey weighs seven to fourteen ounces (200–400 g), which is near the limit of the male's ability to transport it back to the nest. Today, in many regions occupied by nesting peregrines, there is one species that neatly fits the bill: the pigeon. It is far and away the major food in Britain, at inland eyries as well as along the coast. In a sample of just over 4,000 prey remains, which included 106 species, domestic and feral rock doves represented 34 percent! Expressed in percentage of biomass their share would even be greater considering that the sample contained many small passerines weighing less than three ounces (85 g).

Peregrines prefer pigeons for many reasons: they are easy to kill, easy to pluck, well-fleshed and they often fly over open country giving the falcon a fair chance. In eastern North America, as pointed out by Frank Beebe, prior to settlement, the once-abundant passenger pigeon may have been a mainstay of peregrines. Along the northwest coast, nesting Peale's falcons feed primarily on murrelets and auklets that are close to a pigeon in weight. Elsewhere, the peregrine's natural choices are shorebirds and the smaller species of waterfowl. Songbirds are taken opportunistically. Their share increases in wooded habitats and on the barrenlands. In the Arctic of Canada and Greenland, tundra peregrines are dependent upon a sufficient supply of small open-country passerines such as snow buntings. Even nestlings are taken! Surprisingly, Arctic falcons also utilize small mammals such as ground squirrels and lemmings. As reported by Gordon Court, in years when the rodent cycle is high, the abundance of this easy prey allows Keewatin peregrines to expand their breeding population and produce large broods.

The peregrine's menu includes a number of items that may seem odd for a hunter of avian prey. In Britain, wintering peregrines have been seen to kill and eat rabbits! At Beaverhills, I saw a peregrine drop down from a fence post to pick up a vole from the grass. And one day in late May, when the lakeside pastures were covered with a massive hatch of large midges, two immatures behaved like chickens, picking up tiny food items that must have been midges. Insects are in fact a common tidbit for fledglings which enjoy themselves hunting dragonflies, eating them on the wing. More unusual is the fact that peregrines have been recorded to catch fish! Tom Cade once saw a falcon seize an Arctic grayling jumping over an Alaskan river, and Jeremy Tatum watched a peregrine snatch a small sand-lance from the surface of the Pacific Ocean near Victoria. Speaking of singular sightings, Dick Treleaven, a longtime observer of peregrines breeding on the Cornish coast of Britain saw an adult female fly down from her eyrie into a nesting colony of herring gulls and return with a chick which was fed to her young!

To eat crow

Why do peregrines hunt some kinds of prey far more often than others? Is it always a function of numbers and vulnerability? Or could it simply be that some species taste better than others? According to one of Holland's most experienced falconers, his birds demonstrated a strong preference for the meat of pigeon and duck. The phrase "to eat crow" may be derived from falconry. Unless very hungry and humbled by failure to catch more palatable species, few peregrines "stoop so low" as to hunt the black rascals, which are tough and can defend themselves vigorously with their large beak. Although some modern-day falconers train their birds expressly on crows, the wild falcons that I observe very rarely attack them, except for a few playful passes or a threatening stoop in defense of the nest.

Gulls are in another conspicuous and common group of open-country birds within the peregrine's prey range, yet they are not often hunted, at least not at Beaverhills Lake. By contrast, they are taken routinely by the falcons that now nest in central and northern Alberta, perhaps because little else in this weight range is locally available. Nimble flyers such as gulls and terns are hard to catch. Perhaps their fishy taste and oily feathering are disliked as well. However, some individual falcons select the smaller species of gulls nearly exclusively. Specialization in certain kinds of prey, either gulls, pigeons, ducks, shorebirds, passerines or sea birds, is quite typical of peregrines the world over. This may be a question of availability as well as of taste and texture of the flesh.

In contrast to the question of taste, food requirements are much easier to measure and have received their fair share of attention in the hand books. According to information from falconers, three to five ounces (80–150 g) of meat is enough to sustain a peregrine for twenty-four hours. Captive falcons are fed only once a day. If allowed to eat their fill, they will gorge themselves in about twenty-five minutes, storing the meat in the crop or gullet where it is predigested and slowly released into the stomach. Conspicuous in flight, a bulging crop is ample evidence that a falcon has just eaten. A well-fed bird can fast for several days, if it has to. Some authorities claim that a substantial prey item such as a pigeon or duck should last a wild peregrine for two or three days. However, based on my field observations, wintering and migrating falcons kill one or more prey each day. Shorebird hunters consume at least three, and perhaps as many as six, sandpipers daily. Wild peregrines probably have greater appetites than captives and they kill a lot more than they can eat. If large prey are taken, such as ducks, they are shared, willy-nilly, with scavengers. Losses of the entire prey item, just after capture, to pirates such as eagles and buteo hawks are commonplace, forcing the falcon to hunt again.

However, if part of yesterday's prey is still available, peregrines readily return to it in the morning. They will also feed on another falcon's kill and some do not shy away from eating carrion. On Vancouver Island, one winter day, I watched an adult fly down from a high tree perch and alight on the road by a coot that had been killed by traffic! The falcon inspected the flattened carcass and might have utilized it, had not an approaching vehicle forced her to leave. At Beaverhills Lake I saw peregrines feed on the carcasses of ducks that had died from botulism poisoning. Another killed a cripple too weak to lift its head.

Population dynamics

The size of the food resource has a decisive bearing on the dynamics of peregrine populations. The number of eyries on a river or coastline, and the number of young produced, increase or decline with the rise and fall of their prey species. In turn, healthy stocks of prey are dependent on the larger ecosystem. Habitat changes caused by natural factors, such as climate or human activities, can have subtle and not-so-subtle implications for prey and predators alike. After settlement of North America, the large-scale drainage of wetlands must have had a negative impact on peregrines. For instance, the population that used to nest in the Okanagan region of British Columbia disappeared after local marshes had been turned into orchards. Pesticides did not play a role here since the peregrine's disappearance took place during the 1940s, well before the use of agricultural chemicals became widespread.

However, not all land development is bad for the peregrine, which is highly adaptable like most successful, wide-ranging predators. It may even benefit from deforestation and the spread of agriculture if these create a mosaic of habitats that attract a greater mix of prey species than before. Similarly, the building of dams in rivers such as the Colorado have enhanced conditions for several bird species and allowed the peregrine to set up shop in greater densities than before. An even more dramatic example is the fact that this catholic raptor now feels at home in modern cities across the continent.

Unfortunately, other human-related factors affecting the peregrine's welfare are less obvious but can be crucial. The accidental introduction of rats to Langara Island in the Queen Charlottes some decades ago resulted in steep declines of small sea birds that nest on the island's forest floor. It led to a reduction of the prey base for the local peregrines, which became less common than before. Pollution and overfishing are potential future threats to the entire food chain in the Pacific Ocean, including the marine falcons. The species' vulnerability and dependence on healthy prey were at no time more evident than during the pesticide era, which nearly led to the falcon's total demise. Peregrines can also become contaminated with natural afflictions of their prey, such as botulism. If they feed extensively on paralyzed ducks and shorebirds, they risk becoming crippled themselves. Many raptors have been found dead from this endemic and extremely toxic bacterium that can wipe out masses of waterfowl in a matter of days.

Falcons also risk picking up parasites from their prey. Feather lice and mites leaving the dead host can switch to the living. As a counter measure, peregrines love water and bathe often. Walking into the shallows, they splash about and flutter their wings, ridding themselves of some external pests. Unfortunately, internal parasites and pathogens, often acquired from a host species such as pigeons, are harder to shed and may infect a peregrine's throat and crop, leading quickly to death. The fungus *Trichomonas gallinae* or frounce was a common and lethal enemy of captive falcons before the advance of modern medicine. In wild populations the dynamics of disease are little understood. Sublethal effects can contribute to reduced fertility and lifespan. Yet, in spite of these insidious perils, added to the many other often human-caused dangers that threaten the peregrine and its food base, this superlative avian hunter continues to thrive nearly everywhere on this planet!

Chapter 3

Territory and Travels

As the fastest of raptors, peregrines should have few enemies. Yet, there are a number of carnivores, mammals as well as birds, that occasionally make a meal of a falcon. Quite apart from nestling losses to the treacherous great-horned owl, the odd adult falcon, defending its territory, may end up in the clutches of goshawk or eagle. However, in open combat, the peregrine's major enemy is its own kind. On the breeding grounds, pairs fight fiercely over eyrie sites and the chance to procreate, male against male, female against female. In the Canadian Arctic where territoriality has been studied closely by Gordon Court, Mark Bradley and Robin Johnstone, competing falcons of both sexes do not hesitate to strike and grapple with each other, sometimes leading to fatalities. In downtown Edmonton, where peregrine breeding sites are hotly contested each spring, at least two females have been found dead near the nest ledge and partly eaten, probably by the victorious falcon.

Outside the breeding season, intraspecific conflict between peregrines is relentless. Ever jealous, falcons attract falcons. If you watch one of them, sooner or later you'll discover another. He or she may join a hunt in progress or try to steal a kill. During winter, territorial falcons make their most vigorous flights evicting their own kind, usually their own sex. A male and a female, not necessarily a mated pair, may tolerate each other although she might rob him of his prey. Adults also evict and/or rob immatures. The fact that some first-year peregrines starve is because they are excluded from the best hunting grounds, which are dominated by adults.

Competition for food, not for territory, also exists between peregrines and several other predatory birds that take the same species of prey. Piracy, or klepto-parasitism as the experts call it, is a common offense. The more powerful raptors seldom pass up a free meal if they can take it by force from their smaller kin. As detailed in several chapters, the bald eagle is the peregrine's nemesis wherever the two share coastal habitat. This ancient enmity is no longer a fact of life in much of western Europe, where the sea eagle was extirpated centuries ago. There, the female peregrine is now the undisputed queen of birds. Her dapper little king does not lack for enemies, though, even in the eagle's absence. Buteo hawks can constitute a serious nuisance. Also the harrier, if persistent, sometimes manages to chase a tiercel off his catch, forcing him to hunt again.

No better or no worse than its enemies, the peregrine is not above piracy itself. It is quick to commandeer prey from any smaller falcon or hawk. Merlins, kestrels and sharp-shins are just as quick to comply for fear of becoming prey themselves! Peregrines even steal mice from the hard-working harrier! Stooped at repeatedly, the hawk reluctantly jettisons its catch. Half the times the tiny morsel falls into dense vegetation where it is lost to both. In his turn, the smart hawk sometimes gains by following the peregrine. I saw harriers retrieve sandpipers that took cover in grass or reeds after hard pursuit by a falcon. In the same way, the peregrine occasionally benefits from its enemies, for instance when a bald eagle flushes ducks from a pond.

Hurrying home

In temperate and maritime climates, such as along the Pacific Coast, adult peregrines are home bodies that stay all year near their nesting territory, keeping the place occupied and jealously guarded at all times. By contrast, in the Far North they are inveterate travelers that have always bred as close to the permafrost as possible. Like other Arctic migrants, they hurry home each spring to take advantage of the rich food resources, unlimited spaces and long daylight hours of the thawing barrenlands. Their first priority is to establish a territory. Competition can be intense. On the plus side, arch enemies such as the great-horned owl and the bald eagle are absent from the treeless tundra and ice-bound coasts. Serious antagonists such as the gyrfalcon and the golden eagle are few and far between. In favorable weather and with sufficient prey, the peregrine's breeding cycle is completed in the shortest possible time, about three months. Before the brief northern summer has come to an end, the falcons hurry south again. Forced to skip temperate regions, which are occupied by other peregrines, some of these long-range migrants cross the equator to winter deep in South America.

During the few weeks that migration takes place, peregrines can turn up anywhere, although they tend to follow traditional pathways along coastlines, lake shores or mountain ranges. They are not afraid to fly over wide expanses of water. There are numerous reports of falcons alighting on the masts of ships far from land. Some stayed aboard for several days, during which time they made brief forays to hunt small sea birds. The most impressive record is of a peregrine that boarded a freighter 750 miles (1,200 km) west of Africa and disappeared a few days later when it was still more than 600 miles (1,000 km) from South America.

Along the eastern U.S. coast, young peregrines, during their first fall migration, may leave Atlantic headlands to fly to Florida and Cuba over the open ocean, hundreds of miles out at sea. Pushed by tail winds, they remain airborne during the night when warm air currents over the water allow them to soar and sail. This surprising travel pattern was discovered by William Cochran who trapped young falcons on Assateague Island, Maryland, and fitted them with tiny radios attached to a tail feather. The birds were subsequently tracked by means of a light aircraft. Assateague is a hotspot on the fall migration route of peregrines that drift down from the eastern Canadian Arctic and Greenland to their wintering grounds in Central and South America. Along the Atlantic seaboard, they may show up in fair numbers on the beaches of barrier islands, especially if inclement weather forces them to interrupt their journey. Another famous and even better concentration point is South Padre Island on the Gulf of Mexico. Here, hundreds of falcons are captured and banded each fall as well as in spring.

During the return migration, few peregrines tend to follow coastlines and instead hurry home through the heart of the continent, the shortest route to their breeding grounds. On the Alberta plains, as detailed in one of these chapters, migrants pass through from the middle of April to the end of May, long after the local breeders have worked out their territorial conflicts and conquered a corner of a city highrise or a river cliff.

Chapter 4

Return to the River

Sitting on the bank of the Red Deer River, in the dappled shade of a willow stunted by cattle, I am peering through the telescope at the cliffs on the opposite shore. Framed in the circular field of view is an adult tiercel, exquisite and statuesque, his white breast contrasting brightly with the dark background. Changing the angle of the scope, I find the tiercel's mate, crouched down on a grassy ledge lower on the cliff, but all I can see of her are the top of her black head and the glint of an eye.

There has been total peace and quiet for at least two hours. Nothing has stirred in the afternoon heat, except the occasional gull sailing by or a couple of pelicans drifting down on the current. The scenic setting of this prairie river has not changed at all over thirty years, but it is exactly that long ago that I last had the opportunity to focus on a breeding peregrine here. In 1967, after the only remaining nest along this Alberta river had failed to fledge young, the population became extirpated. Their local disappearance had been caused by the destructive activities of mankind. Now, in 1997, the falcon's return was again entirely due to the intervention of humans, through the efforts of a few dedicated individuals who, with the support of government agencies, conservation organizations and corporate sponsors, had raised and released captive young. And the first falcons to come back as adults to nest on the Red Deer had chosen the very same cliff site that was the last to be occupied three decades earlier!

Both members of this pair were banded on the left leg with a silver-colored ring, and on the right leg with a bright red one, coded with two white letters. Through a powerful telescope, Rob Corrigan of the Alberta Fish and Wildlife Division was able to identify the tiercel: X over D. Checking back with government records, he reported that this particular falcon had been raised at the Wainwright breeding facility in Alberta, and that it had been hacked out two years ago, together with his mate, along this very same river a few miles downstream. Yet, the pair behaved as if their kind had been here for generations. Programmed by millennia of evolution, their genes included the precise command to do what was required of them to perpetuate their species. Upon reflection, it seems nothing short of a miracle that these falcons, hatched in an incubator and raised by foster parents in a flight pen, knew unfailingly what to do. It was as if they had never been away, as if the chain had never been broken. These falcons had proven to be vulnerable, yet they were also resilient and adaptable, bouncing back with vigor now that the environmental hazards had been reduced. For me, it was a new chance to observe this celebrated species at its nest, an opportunity that not long ago had seemed for ever past.

The cliff as magnet

Riding the wind, a mere speck in the wide prairie sky, the falcon's perspective is unlimited: a vast panorama of tilting fields and pastures, studded with dugouts and sloughs, stretching to the blue horizon. Watching the soaring bird through binoculars, I am mesmerized by his artistry as he draws quick elliptical loops across the bulging cumulus of spring. He seems the embodiment of boundless freedom, yet he is tied by a life line to a steep river bank far below, where a vertical wall of exposed sandstone juts out of the otherwise wooded, north-facing slope. Soon he will fold his wings and come home in a singing stoop.

The world over, peregrines have a few basic and particular requirements. They depend on rocky escarpments that command a wide view of open landscapes rich in prey. The best cliffs draw them like a magnet, generation after generation. Next to an adequate food base, the availability of suitable nesting sites, usually overlooking water, is a major factor determining the size of peregrine populations everywhere. Unlike other raptors, peregrines do not build a nest. They require at least one suitable ledge on the cliff, ideally with an overhang that offers protection from the elements as well as from mammalian raiders. In regions devoid of cliffs, the odd falcon may use an abandoned stick nest, constructed by buteos or ravens in an isolated tree.

In Finnish and Russian wetlands, peregrines resort to hummocks in moorland or marshes. Like all true falcons, they do nothing to furnish their eyrie. They simply scrape a shallow depression in the gravely substrate or duff, large enough to contain a set of eggs.

In defense of their home site, peregrines fight ferociously with competitors. Their battle cry is a strident and repetitious *cack-cack-cack...* that carries far. They also chase off other raptors, magpies and ravens that might pose a threat to the future safety of eggs or young. The fury of an angry peregrine in defense of its home is a sight to behold! Some do not hesitate to strike potential enemies such as dogs and eagles, and many a researcher has been welcomed with a bloody scratch on his skull!

On the nest ledge

Ever vigilant, soaring and sailing high over the valley, the pair court each other with undulating stoops and playful pursuits. If their cliff has more than one ledge, the birds inspect several and entice their partner to have a look before the final selection is made. Bowing to each other, they vocalize excitedly with clucking *ee-chup* calls. Copulation takes place on perches near the eyrie. Tilting forward invitingly, she turns her back toward him and raises her tail at a steep angle. He lands on her with closed feet, balancing with extended wings, and bending his tail sideways to achieve cloacal contact. Like all birds, the male lacks an external sex organ and copulation is not always successful at the first try. However, the pair comes together a number of times each day, most frequently during the morning.

Gradually, the female becomes lethargic, spending more and more time on the ledge. She stops hunting and begs the male for food like a young chick with quivering wings and plaintive calls. If hungry, she may even charge him aggressively, stimulating him to go hunting. If he returns with food, usually a small bird, he may land on a ledge and present the item to her in his bill, or he may transfer it in midair as she flies upward below him. The event always appears to excite them and is accompanied by much calling. For a bird that is a loner for most of the year and repels other falcons as rivals, the close cooperation required during food transfer and copulation means a profound change in attitude.

Peregrine eggs are somewhat smaller and rounder than a medium chicken egg. They vary from golden brown to reddish in color and are beautifully decorated. Few are exactly the same. In the past they were highly prized by collectors, who obtained series of sets from different regions. Fortunately, this harmful hobby has declined in popularity, largely because of protective legislation. Eggs are produced at intervals of two or three days and the clutch is complete at four, sometimes one more or less. Incubation begins soon after the third one is laid, although Arctic breeders may cover the eggs at once. The female does most of the incubating, including at night, but the male takes his turn to keep the eggs warm while she is feeding or preening, until she is ready to resume the boring task.

The great moment arrives after about five weeks. Chirping softly inside the egg, as if to announce its arrival, the chick works hard to pip and break the shell with its tiny bill, taking days of effort. It finally emerges, wet and exhausted, to be covered warmly by the fluffed-out breast feathers of mother. It is one of nature's heartwarming miracles that even rapacious and belligerent predators such as peregrines turn into tender care-givers as soon as their young enter the world.

The functional family

The task of rearing the young is shared by both parents and they have complementary duties. The male supplies the female with food for herself and their offspring. Meeting him in the air or on a ledge to receive his offering, she takes the carcass back to the nest. Tearing it up with her bill, she offers the most appetizing morsels to the young. When tiny, they are well-behaved and sit in a semicircle in front of her. Between them there is a minimum of fighting, and each of them receives its share.

Except when being fed, the small young are brooded almost continuously. They huddle together for warmth and spend most of their time dozing. But after two weeks or so, when their sparse whitish down is replaced with a coarser coat, they are only covered during cold, rainy periods or shaded from hot sun. The female now spends less time with her progeny and begins to make forays over the hunting range. In her absence, the male may attend to the chicks, feeding them in the same careful manner as his mate. At other times, he just does not feel like it and waits for her return. Holding the fresh-ly caught prey in his feet, he sits on a high perch, all the while scan-ning the horizon. As soon as he sees his mate approaching, he meets her at once on the nest. In times of abundance, the female may decline his offering and the tiercel caches it as surplus food on a ledge where he or she retrieves it when needed. If well-fed, growth of the young continues at a phenomenal rate, their weight increas-ing more than twenty times their hatching weight. Large females gain the most. Starting out at about one ounce (28 g) when they emerge from the egg, they end up at two pounds (0.9 kg) or more, an increase of thirty-two times in about forty-four days!

The growth of feathers starts out from the same follicles as the down, pushing it out as a fluffy flag on the tip of the feather until it falls off. By the third week, wing primaries form and facial feathers lend color to the head. As their independent nature awakens, they explore as far as the ledge allows. Soon they can feed themselves and the adults just drop the food onto the ledge, avoiding close contact with their increasingly assertive charges. At five to six weeks of age, the young are practically fully feathered except for some wisps of clownish down sticking to their head, flanks and rump. They preen a lot and may even do some mutual preening. Exercising their grow-ing muscles, they stand on the edge of the nest ledge and flap their stubby wings. The females are bigger than their brothers, which develop a little faster. The tiercels are the first to take wing, on some windy day.

After fledging, the juveniles turn into greedy monsters that harass the adults relentlessly, even if they have just eaten their fill. Screaming and begging in typical flutter-glide, they mercilessly accost their parents. Steve Sherrod saw fledglings thrust both claws into their mother's chest or grab hold of her wing. To avoid them, the adults perch well away from the eyrie. Scrapping and chasing each other, the young also harass any other bird that comes within range, even large ones such as herons and geese. Riding the wind, they practice their footwork by grabbing at the fluttering leaves of trees or flowers. Spending hours soaring at great heights, they grad-ually expand their range, following their parents to their hunting grounds. Their first self-caught food items are usually insects, such as dragonflies, which are eaten on the wing.

Learning as they go

The question of how young falcons master their trade has been raised by many observers. It has been demonstrated beyond question that juveniles can manage without instruction. Their innate hunting skills have proven themselves over and over again during the past two decades when hundreds of captive-raised young were released from hack-sites and survived to become adults. All they needed were four to six weeks of guaranteed access to food while they progressed from dependency to self-reliance. However, there is no doubt that youngsters raised by wild parents do receive a certain amount of instruction, even if it occurs only indirectly or inadvertently. Adult falcons have been seen to release dead or live prey in the air for their flying young. If the pursuing juvenile fails to catch the item, the adult stoops to retrieve it and repeats the procedure. Whether or not this proves that adults deliberately teach their young is a moot point. The release of live prey may simply be prompted by the hurried approach of aggressive young. Any peregrine carrying a prey is at a disadvantage if set upon by a conspecific. To get away it may be forced to surrender its catch.

Dick Treleaven, at nest sites on the west coast of Britain, and Saul Frank by the suspension bridges of New York, have written lively accounts of fledglings joining their parents in the hunt. If the adult captures a pigeon, it is released dead or alive for the approaching juveniles. Such cooperative forays may be quite routine, although they are not often observed, perhaps because most breeding pairs hunt away from the nesting cliff. Years ago, I had a brief opportunity to watch fledgling peregrines on Lake Athabasca in northern Alberta. One evening the adults took off from a tree perch above the eyrie cliff and began a long chase of a juvenile black tern over the water. To my surprise, the pair was joined by one of their young, which made several swoops in the same manner as its parents. Incredibly, after minutes of hot pursuit, the dodging tern escaped and found cover in dense willows.

More recently, in 1998, I saw a lot of family fun at Lake Wabamun in central Alberta. The three young, fledged a few weeks earlier from a nest box attached to the smoke stack of a powerplant, were eager to join their parents in action. They dive-bombed gulls that the adults had forced down in a pond, and they alternated with the tiercel swooping at shorebirds and passerines far out over the lake. These exploits are described in more detail in chapter fourteen.

Fledglings learn by trial and error as well as by imitating their parents and each other. This goes for hunting as well as for other essential life skills such as recognizing and avoiding a wide variety of hazards. The period of fledging is the final stage of the nesting cycle, deciding the pair's productivity and the future of their genes.

As a hedge against the slim odds of juvenile survival, nature has endowed the peregrine with adequate fecundity. Reaching breeding age in their second year, some even in their first, barely twelve months after hatching, a pair can fledge two to five young per season. However, the vast majority do not get such an early chance if the competition for territories is severe. The maximum age of wild adults has been recorded as eighteen or nineteen years. In captivity, some birds have reached an age of up to twenty-six. Regardless of the fairly high nest failure rate, caused by a range of factors, natural and unnatural, healthy breeding populations average roughly two young per pair, which is more than enough to maintain their number. Researchers have noted that missing adults are replaced quickly. The surviving partner soon attracts a new mate. Thus, there must be a substantial floating reserve of nonbreeders, despite the fact that adult mortality is calculated at 10–30 percent per year. Based on banding returns, juvenile mortality is even higher; well over half do not survive their first winter!

Drifting south in early fall over unknown country, immature birds need to locate and hold a good winter hunting ground, competing with each other and aggressive adults for the best habitats. In populated regions, they may be shot or critically wounded by colliding with obstacles such as power lines. On top of all that, some even kill themselves by a split-second miscalculation in what they do for a living, stooping at prey! There are several reports of falcons that failed to put on the brakes in time and slammed into the ground, suffering massive injuries. This celebrated bird, fastest creature in the world, that lives by violence, frequently dies by violence.

Chapter 5

Watcher at the Lake

Weaving its way through a stiff head wind, the migrating pere-grine follows the open west side of Beaverhills Lake, a shallow but huge sheet of water, eleven miles (18 km) across its longest axis. At the north end, where the shore curves east, the falcon descends and finds a resting spot among the waving tussocks of foxtail on a cow pasture. Seeking shelter from the breeze, the tired bird does not mind sitting low on the ground; its destination and ancestral home are the flat Arctic tundra where trees are absent, cliffs few and far between. It has come a long way, returning from winter ranges in South America. Faded by tropical sun, its plumage matches the color of dry grass. It is a first-year bird; the pale chest and belly are thinly streaked and the back is a sandy brown. Even the top of its head is flecked with light brown. How different it looks from the brightly colored adults that followed this same migration route one or two weeks earlier! It is now well past the middle of May, but this young female is in no hurry. She will not be of breeding age until at least one more year has passed.

The falcon rests for an hour or so, but her head is never still—the brilliant eyes scanning the landscape and the sky above. By focusing, she can make a distant speck flare up into sharp detail. Suddenly, she takes wing. Following the lake shore at a steady pace, she skims the winter-ravaged cattails and dips low over the mudflats. Blackbirds raise a chorus of alarm. Godwits, avocets and killdeer shrill into the sky. Loafing ducks rush to water. Nearly a mile away in less than one minute, the falcon is lost to sight. Flocks of sand-pipers and gulls rise like smoke over fire, silver and white against the darkening sky.

Chilled and stiff after the long wait in the lee of a willow bush, I trudge back to the road. Just before reaching the car, I halt for a final scan of lakeside pastures and fields. The wind has increased to a gusty squall that makes it hard to steady the glasses. The eastern sky is black. To the south, over a golden stubble field lit by a ray of low sun, a peregrine, tiny and sharply outlined, races downwind at tremendous speed. Suddenly, it shoots upward like a rocket to meet a string of birds head-on. The falcon slams into one of them and grappled together they plummet steeply to the ground, out of view.

The incident took place so furiously fast and far away that I am left wondering what exactly happened. Was it really a peregrine? And had it just captured a duck? Or was it a merlin taking a black-bird? The birds had looked so small.... After a moment of hesitation, despite threatening rain, I quickly decide to check it out. Halting briefly from time to time, I scan the ground ahead but see nothing until the falcon suddenly flies up from behind a slight rise in the ground. It is an adult, blue-backed and white-chested, quite unlike the brownish bird seen earlier! And she is big, obviously a female. Cackling in protest, she circles, then leaves. On the spot from where she flushed I find the remains of a shoveler drake, neck and breast bloody and partly consumed. The grass is strewn with a wind vane of white and brown feathers.

When I began my observations at Beaverhills Lake in central Alberta, way back in 1964, next to nothing was known about the spring migration of peregrines in North America. Few were seen in the interior of the continent. Around the lake, local birdwatchers recorded the occasional sighting during May when the passage of Arctic migrants is at its peak. It is an exciting time, when wave after wave of waterfowl and shorebirds touches down during a relatively brief span of time. Each spring, the long winter finally past, I revel in the return of avian life, but there is one species I want to see more than any other bird: the peregrine. And above all I want to see it hunt. But that took a lot of patient and deliberate effort over many years. During my first spring at the lake I could count the total of falcon sightings on the fingers of one hand, but gradually my yearly score increased tenfold. By being in the field from dawn to dusk, seven days a week, I learned when and how to look. And little by little, one observation at a time, I began to understand the peregrine's ecology. The following pages describe its migratory routines and foraging strategies: how it sets out to capture the shifty sandpipers and the swiftest of ducks, and how these much-hunted prey species manage to cope with an enemy as dangerous as the bolt from the blue.

Soaring to the clouds

The spring migration of peregrines, hurrying north, takes place in any kind of weather but they are most likely to be seen on overcast days with southerly breezes, heralding the arrival of a cold front. When the wind shifts to the north and rain settles in, the falcons descend. Flying low along the shore, they are easy to spot. Some may stay awhile in the area and not resume their journey until the sky clears.

In the morning, beginning its day leisurely, the well-fed peregrine rests on a fence post or stone, preening its feathers and watching other birds go by. A mob of crows or a cheeky harrier may swoop irritatingly close, but the falcon is reluctant to flush until the sun has warmed the air. When other hawks are beginning to soar, the peregrine stirs from its lethargy, stretching its wings in an almost sensual manner. Folding them again, it sits for another spell until the urge to migrate can no longer be suppressed. Opening its wings once more and briefly holding them fully extended, it jumps lightly off its post. Flapping briskly, it drops low over the ground at first, then climbs into the wind. Feeling a thermal, it stops beating and spreads its tail. Carried by a column of rising air, the falcon drifts downwind, perhaps in a direction different from its intended travel route. Circling at a rate of speed greater than other soaring hawks, it rises higher and higher until it can barely be seen through binoculars. After it stops soaring, reaching the top of the thermal, it sets its wings slightly back and narrows the tail. Cutting through the wind at increasing speed, it glides into a northwesterly direction, vanishing in the cloud-studded vastness of the prairie sky.

It took many seasons of watching before I understood this common morning routine. At the time my observations began, it was generally thought that peregrines always traveled at low or moderate altitudes. To see them soar to great heights was an exciting discovery, the reward of observing resting falcons during the morning until they flew off. Sometimes it took several hours and it was actually disappointing just to see the birds depart, because the reason I watched them in the first place was to observe them hunt. Therefore, I was all the more pleased when I found out later that high altitude soaring was not only the way they migrated, it also proved to be a deadly hunting strategy. And this had not been reported in the scientific literature either.

Strategies

Searching for peregrines, I walked the lakeside pastures and frequently stopped to scan the area ahead through binoculars. Alerted by alarm behavior of shorebirds, I might catch a distant glimpse of a falcon but its attack on prey was usually finished. All it did was disappear from sight. By the time I had reached the area where the disturbance had taken place, flocks of shorebirds were rising again far away, indicating where the next hunt had just occurred. It seemed that I was always in the wrong place at the wrong time.

This frustrating and unproductive scenario improved after I began using some strategy myself. Instead of running after the falcon, I decided to let the falcon come to me. And the way to do that was to join the prey. Sitting down quietly on a stone by the lake, I spent hours just looking around and enjoying the scenery. After a while, the shorebirds approached closely, foraging for shrimps and insect larvae in the shallows or for midges in the short grass. While I marveled at the details of their plumage, my ears were attuned to their calls. At a distant alarm, they cocked their heads and watched the sky, crouching motionless. Sharing their excitement and their fears, I involuntarily hunched my shoulders in apprehension. If the birds resumed feeding, I searched the skies through binoculars, focusing on clouds, and sometimes I found the peregrine, a minuscule anchor-shaped dot, wings spread, tips blunted by distance. If it left the white background of cloud and soared into the blue, the bird was beyond the unaided eye, hidden by height, just a blurry speck in the glasses.

A soaring peregrine that pulls in its wings reduces its outline further to a circle not much bigger than the circumference of its body.

Falling straight at its target, the round dot dilates at a deceptively slow rate until it flares up with a roar of wings, talons flashing. Anyone who has stood near an eyrie and has experienced the headlong stoop of an enraged falcon, aimed at one's head, can appreciate the terror that this predator strikes into the heart of little birds.

The final act of grabbing a shorebird is a split-second hit or miss, usually taking place close to the ground where vegetation or heat haze make it all the more difficult to see exactly what happens. Visibility during the critical last stage of the attack often leaves much to be desired. It may only be possible to learn whether or not the falcon was successful if subsequent behavior provides a clue. If the bird flies up with empty feet and resumes soaring, it is clear that the hunt failed. If it alights and begins feeding, it obviously scored. Quite often peregrines made their kill nearby while I was looking the other way. Even if I was alerted by the hiss of their stoop, I could miss seeing the actual strike. To discover the attacking falcon in time, you have to be not only in the right place at the right time, you also have to be looking in the right direction!

My luck improved after I fine-tuned my strategy. Instead of sitting close by the shore, I kept my distance and selected a spot from where I could keep an eye on two or more areas with a concentration of shorebirds. When panic struck in one area, I searched the sky in the hope of finding the falcon before it launched an attack in the other.

Bolt from the blue

One of the first hunts that I observed in complete detail unfolded while I was sitting by a fence line along a high field that allowed a panoramic view of the lake. It was early May. The ice had just broken up. Floes were pushed into glittering bergs onto the downwind shore. The water was still too cold to sustain much aquatic life, and the shorebirds, which had just arrived, were feeding in wet fields and meadows. From my vantage point I could watch two areas of floodwater, crowded with ducks, yellowlegs and pectoral sandpipers. When the birds flushed and drew together in dense flocks over one wetland, I glassed the sky and was thrilled to pick up an adult falcon, large enough to be a female. She began to soar, wafting higher after every circle, drifting farther away. After five or ten minutes, I could barely distinguish her, a tiny speck high over inland woods. Was she leaving on migration? Hoping fervently that she would come back, I leaned against a fence post to steady my arms and waited. The falcon stopped circling and glided back upwind. Slowly, almost imperceptibly, her minuscule silhouette grew and darkened. Poised straight over me at last, seen through ten-power glasses, she looked as small as a mosquito, her altitude perhaps close to a mile (1.6 km). By now I had been watching her for about half an hour. My arms and neck were aching. Changing position ever so carefully, I managed to keep her in my circular view.

Suddenly, she tilted over. The late afternoon sun lit up her underside like a flash of gold and she was gone, instantly, as if she had burned up, extinguished like a meteor entering the atmosphere. Dumbfounded I searched the empty sky, until I realized that she must have stooped. Over the nearest wetland shorebirds were rising in dense flocks. Beyond them, the falcon was leaving already, climbing back up into the wind with quick sculling wingbeats.

Relieved that she had obviously not been successful, and hoping that she would make another attack, I kept her in view until she was once more poised high overhead. When she finally keeled over, she stooped perpendicularly, revolving, piercing golden through blue sky and black through white cloud. Near the ground, she drew level and raced low toward the water, abruptly shooting up at a steep angle. A single sandpiper flushed below her. She stooped and caught it at once. Landing on a fence post, she plucked her prey. Twenty minutes later, she left again and circled up to a great height, until she set her sights on the northwest.

Taken by surprise

Since that memorable day, I have observed hundreds of other peregrines hunt in much the same style. Between spells of soaring, some stooped half a dozen times before making a kill. In the last stage of their plunge, they zoomed horizontally over land or water, ready to seize sandpipers that rose directly in their path. If the prey flushed well ahead and had attained top speed, it might be chased but seldom for long. Giving up after one or two passes, the falcon returned to the clouds and tried its luck elsewhere, again counting on the element of surprise.

As other observers have noted, peregrines often seem to attack out of the sun, like fighter pilots during the war years. The question of whether or not falcons do so deliberately is something else. Perhaps they naturally follow that angle since it creates the best light conditions. However, the fact that the prey's sight is partially blocked by the glare enhances the falcon's chance for surprise at close range. Yet, even these blinding strikes fail nine out of ten times. Sandpipers have an amazing ability to dodge even the most sudden surprise attack. With split-second reflex, they drop down and take off at once in the opposite direction. Overshooting the mark, the falcon usually flies on, but sometimes it brakes hard over a plunging sandpiper. If it flushes at once, the falcon swoops down in pursuit. Prey that stay down are quickly picked up from the ground. It is quite possible that some of these birds were raked by the falcon's claws during the initial pass, although I could seldom be sure. As mentioned earlier, just once was I close enough to see that a sandpiper had obviously been struck dead since it ended up floating motionlessly on the water. By contrast, in many other cases I clearly saw that a sandpiper dropped down before the falcon got near enough to touch it and that the peep took off again the moment its attacker had passed by. During this split-second routine of near-hits and narrow escapes, sandpipers often plunge into water. Some take off again at once. Others try to evade the falcon's next pass by splashing aside. A few even manage to get away after several unsuccessful passes. Those that hesitate are doomed.

Peregrines are very good at plucking prey from the water's surface. In one exceptional case I saw an adult tiercel retrieve a shorebird that had totally submerged. This adult male, in a surprise attack over a shallow slough, flushed a small flock of dowitchers. One of them plunged back and disappeared completely under water, perhaps holding on to the bottom. Like a kingfisher, the tiercel hovered about twelve feet (4 m) above the surface for a few seconds. He then dived in up to his belly, feet first, and came up carrying the dowitcher. All this happened quite close by, giving me a perfect view of this rare incident!

Surprise is also the ultimate objective in other hunting methods, such as high altitude flapping flight. Cruising along at a steady pace, the falcon looks far ahead. When prey is sighted, it descends obliquely, flattening out in a shallow stoop, alternating with bursts of wingbeats quivering close to the tail. This is very exciting to watch! The terminal stage of the attack is low over ground or water, giving resting or feeding prey the fright of their lives.

During inclement weather and in late evening, hunting pere-grines skim very fast over the lake shore and in between the reed beds, mile after mile. They attempt to seize prey opportunistically on the ground or just after it flushes ahead. Resting from time to time, hungry falcons continue their low coursing flight until well after sun-down, their basic strategy of surprise enhanced by the deepening dark.

Safety in numbers

By the middle of May, migratory sandpipers can build up along Beaverhills Lake to tens of thousands, depending on the availability of mudflat habitat and the abundance of food. Under favorable weather conditions, the hatch of chironomid midges is incredible. During calm periods, they swarm like a curtain of smoke over the reeds and pastures. Wind forces them down, clinging to vegetation. Then, the sandpipers move out onto the grass and become even more vulnerable since their view of the surroundings is obscured and their enemy can approach unseen.

Perched on a fence post or soaring high among the clouds, pere-grines spy on their prey from afar. From time to time, they make stealth attacks at top speed low over the pastures, flushing their prey just ahead. But not all sandpipers rise. They freeze instead, reacting instinctively to the alarm calls of other birds. The least sandpiper, with its dark and striped back, relies on camouflage and often crouches motionlessly on bare mud. The pectoral sandpiper feels safer in the grass and may also crouch. If the falcon had spotted the birds from afar, it seems to be puzzled by their disappearance. Flying slowly, head bent down, it may search for them, quartering the ground like a harrier.

The overall success rate in 439 surprise hunts was close to 10 percent, but if the falcon aimed its attacks on lone prey or isolated small flocks, its success rose significantly to 24 percent! By contrast, when there were masses of shorebirds everywhere, the falcon's capture rate dropped to 6 percent. Its approach is then nearly always noticed in time by nontarget birds. Locally breeding species such as the marbled godwit are intensely watchful, standing tall and craning its long neck to look over the vegetation. As soon as it cries *hawk*, all sandpipers secure their getaway. I watched adult falcons make ten or fifteen aborted stealth attacks in succession, frustrated by early alarms. Well before they reached their intended prey, birds flushed far and near. There is clearly safety in numbers! It is exactly for this reason, to minimize the danger of being taken by surprise, that prey species flock together. It is also why shorebirds prefer an open habitat since it allows them to spot their enemies from afar. If both these conditions are met—great numbers and wide-open spaces—the hunter can no longer rely entirely on its strategy of surprise. It has to compensate with persistence and selectivity. It is then that we have a chance to see the peregrine at its best, in a fair chase, striving to outperform a prey that is a close match in speed.

Hot pursuit

Even on the widest mudflats, the peregrine tries to get as close as possible before being detected, either after a terrific stoop, an oblique descent from far away or a low stealth flight. However, the first pass is bound to fail. While the sky fills with fleeing shorebirds, the falcon mounts, in plain view to all. Turning and descending in a burst of speed, it selects a single sandpiper flying lower than the others. Overtaken rapidly, the sandpiper may be seized directly from behind. However, far and away the majority twist aside at the last moment. Unless the falcon gives up at once, it regains altitude and repeats the downward rush at the same target. It does not stoop with wings fully pulled in. Instead it descends at an oblique angle while flapping furiously. If it misses, it shoots back up just as steeply, flying in vertical zigzags, all the while beating its wings. As long as the peregrine has the advantage of superior height, it is astounding how quickly it overhauls a fleeing sandpiper. However, the falcon's swoops are straight and hugely overpowered, every time leaving a wide gap separating prey from predator. Before its enemy has managed to turn around, the sandpiper has changed course, often into the opposite direction, enlarging the distance separating the two. More often than not the falcon soon abandons the chase.

The peregrine's chances are much better if the sandpiper stays low or is forced even lower after several swoops. Demoralized, it may head for shore and drop into any available cover or it may splash down into the water. Unable to dive, sandpipers are vulnerable over the lake, which is exactly why the peregrine is keen to hunt them there, even if the eventual capture may take numerous swoops. Long chases have a high success rate of about 18 percent but are costly in terms of energy. With such tiny prey, the return in calories is low. I have often seen peregrines resume hunting sandpipers immediately after eating one.

The tundra falcon show

Persistence is typical of the smallish immature peregrines of the *tundrius* variety that arrive at the lake by the second week of May. High spirited, they fall from the sky like meteors and soar back up with astonishing ease on any wind. Their silhouette is very slender. Typically, their narrow wings show a slight curve at the carpal joint, like a gull's. If food is plentiful, some of these immatures linger at the lake until well into the second half of May. They have no urgent reason to push on northward, since they are not yet of breeding age. They spend a lot of time on the wing. It seems, at least to me, that they hunt sandpipers for the sheer joy of it as well as for food. They persist in long chases even if it takes dozens of swoops before they obtain their reward. They are like gourmets, indulging in their favorite pastime, not in a hurry to eat their fill and end the party. Quite often a peregrine in hot pursuit of a sandpiper is joined by others. They attack alternately, swooping and climbing back up with abandon, twenty or thirty times. I have counted a combined total of fifty swoops before the prey was caught or got away. In one case, I saw five peregrines pursue the same sandpiper high over the lake. A sixth arrived just too late.

Migrating on the same weather systems as the shorebirds, the number of peregrines is greatest when their prey are most common. Among themselves the falcons quarrel frequently. A joint hunt is not so much a matter of cooperation as it is of competition, of taking advantage of the other guy's effort. They are intensely jealous and the females always try to rob the males. The successful tiercel climbs away at once and heads far inland to eat his prey. Or he eats on the wing. Soaring high in the blue, on still wings, he brings the prey forward and bends his head down. Looking up at his tiny silhouette through binoculars, you can see plucked feathers drift away like puffs of white smoke.

The last, and most fantastic, spectacle of spring migration at the lake is what I call the falcon and phalarope show. A plump little bird that seeks its food while swimming but is unable to dive, the red-necked phalarope can be extremely numerous, collecting by the thousands, often well away from shore. At the approach of a falcon, the flock veers and gyrates, trying to shake the enemy. As more falcons arrive, other flocks balloon into the sky. Under attack, their reaction becomes ever more violent, surging up or sweeping down like a writhing snake low over the water. All the while, falcons, like black boomerangs, attack in vertical zigzags. If they isolate and pursue a single bird, far out over the lake, the tiny target may be invisible from shore. For this reason, it was very hard to tell whether or not the falcons I watched were successful. Although I picked up a few peregrines carrying their phalarope back to land, I had not seen these particular birds hunting so that I could not add these prey captures to my growing list of kills.

Beginner's luck

The spectacular falcon and phalarope show far out over the lake usually escapes the attention of local birdwatchers. To find peregrines, one has to know their habits and even then most may be missed. Very often I have watched from a distance as falcons flew right by or over people who did not notice them. (Since I have no eyes in the top of my head or in my neck, I sometimes get the feeling that I fail to spot more falcons than I see!) However, groups of birders peering through telescopes to identify distant shorebirds can even remain unaware of falcons that make an attack nearby. The general uproar of rising flocks distracts attention and obscures the culprit's getaway. Despite their open environment, falcons easily escape notice or are dismissed as just another hawk if they sit quietly on a stone or fence post in the distance. Moreover, the best days to see peregrines at the lake are wet and windy when few birders are in the field. If the sky clears, people return but most peregrines have left. Nevertheless, some keen birders have reported the capture of prey right in front of their noses on days when my efforts produced little or nothing. Always a matter of chance, the most unusual sightings can be a matter of beginner's luck.

When I was still a novice peregrine watcher, I saw some things I have never seen since. For instance, I once saw a low-flying falcon grabbing a bird out of a wet sedge meadow, holding it by the head and carrying it along without stopping. I never found out the species of the prey; it was probably a lesser yellowlegs or perhaps a sora rail, a secretive denizen of the marsh. Another early observation still remains the only incident of a peregrine dashing right into a dense flock of sandpipers and emerging with a prey in its talons.

Flocking is a collective antipredator strategy resulting from the desire of individual birds to seek shelter in the middle of the group. The closer the danger, the tighter the group. Pressing together in a roar of small wings, a flock of sandpipers takes on the shape of a perfect sphere, a dynamic mass of bodies that discourages all but the boldest enemies.

That rare incident happened one evening, when an immature female peregrine made a pass at a flock of about sixty buff-breasted sandpipers which flushed in alarm from ploughland. Flying on and alighting on a fence post by the shore, one mile away, the falcon could just be seen as a tiny black dot against the water. She sat there until after sunset. When she finally left the post, she approached low over the fields, almost invisible against the dark background until she rose over the skyline. Winging hard, she continued to climb and suddenly the sandpipers came into view, ascending like a tightly packed ball, dark against the bright, unclouded sky. The sun was just below the horizon, but the flock went so high that it was touched by a ray of light and transformed into a luminous golden globe. At that very moment, the falcon slammed into her target like an exploding shell, sandpipers scattering like fiery sparks. Grabbing her prey point-blank, the falcon glided down to a corner of the dusky field. I decided not to disturb her. Next morning I searched for the remains and held the feathers of the sandpiper in my hands, tangible proof of the fantastic, almost surreal observation that was undoubtedly one of the most spectacular shorebird hunts I have ever seen at the lake.

Incidentally, I owed the above unique experience to a novice birdwatcher who was kind and patient enough to keep his telescope glued on the tiny dot of the falcon sitting on the distant post. He alerted me to the bird's departure. Regrettably, after he put his scope aside and aimed his binoculars, he could not relocate the falcon himself until after the kill had been made. No beginner's luck for him!

Chapter 6

A Mixed Bag

The check list of wading birds at Beaverhills Lake includes three dozen species. However, very few of these fall prey to peregrines. Those that take the brunt of predation are the most numerous, such as the pectoral sandpiper. Plovers, seemingly in a better weight range, are rarely taken unless alone or in a small isolated flock. The conspicuous black-bellied plover and its much more cryptic cousin, the golden plover, are usually the first to call alarm and take to the air. Other large waders are just as wary, particularly those that nest locally. The avocet, despite its loud plumage, always escapes the falcon's clutches. Killdeer, willet and marbled godwit never seem to be caught, although I found the odd plucked remains and one day I actually witnessed the death of a godwit, the most alert of all prairie sentinels. Implicated in this little lakeside drama was an immature male peregrine, but he did not make the kill. He had, however, aimed a high-spirited stoop at the godwit. Thereafter, the latter hunkered down in the grass and watched the soaring predator warily, mesmerized by his circling high in the sky. I too was watching the tiercel which made other mock attacks here and there. Presently, he swooped down at a red-tailed hawk sitting in the grass, mantling over a prey. It proved to be the godwit! The hawk must have glided down unseen from behind and grabbed its unsuspecting victim while its eye was on the peregrine!

Snow buntings on my head

In April, before the arrival of transient shorebirds, male peregrines hunt passerines, particularly snow buntings, which can be locally numerous. Swarming over the stubble fields, their flocks proceed in a peculiar roll-over fashion. The last to rise pass over the vanguard that has already landed to grab a quick bite to eat. The relentless nervousness of these pretty birds is due to fear of the hawk. Apart from the peregrine, they are hunted hard by merlins and harriers. Even sharp-shinned and Swainson's hawks may take a crack at them, dropping out of the sky like falling stones.

Here too, the peregrine's main strategy is surprise. Spying on the buntings from a great height, it carefully chooses the moment when the harassed flocks are down for a minute. One adult tiercel attacked in a classic stoop and leveled out low over the ground. He grabbed a bird just as the flock lifted like a wall of white wings off the stubble. Another tiercel savaged a flock until the desperate little birds took cover on a huge stack of ice floes piled up by the wind on the lake shore. In his final descent, after a prolonged spell of soaring, the tiercel stooped in a measured way and slowed down just enough to pluck his victim, frozen with fear, from the surface of the ice. The other buntings stayed down, white on white.

On another eventful day, with snow buntings everywhere, two adult tiercels were terrorizing flocks over inland fields while I was standing by my parked car. Leaning my elbows on the roof I was watching the distant action through glasses. After some time, both falcons soared overhead and began a terrific series of attacks on flocks nearby. Dozens of buntings, seeking cover, rained down on my (white) car, and a few clamped their toes on my head and shoulders!

As with the shorebirds, the brunt of predation on passerines is taken by the migrants. By comparison, species that breed locally in large numbers, such as blackbirds, seem rather immune from the peregrine, secure in their habitat of choice. Immature falcons are fond of chasing red-wings hither and thither over the reeds although I never saw one caught. Other grassland passerines, such as meadowlarks and savannah sparrows may be attacked on an opportunistic basis but are seldom taken. Curiously, in thirty-three years of walking along the lake I have just once found the remains of a pigeon, a worldwide peregrine staple, which is not uncommon around area farms but scarce by the shore.

The shifty gulls

All but ignoring most of the locally breeding birds, the migrant pere-grines that pass through central Alberta in April and May are occa-sionally tempted by resident gulls and terns, which are numerous. However, these buoyant flyers are difficult to catch. If an immature peregrine gives it a try, it usually becomes a great show! Whether or not the falcon is serious or just having some fun at the expense of the gull is hard to say. Attacked from above, Franklin's and Bonaparte's gulls shift aside to evade the stoop and mount steeply again with an anxious scream. Their terror increases if the peregrine persists, especially if two or more falcons cooperate and alternately swoop at the same gull, twenty or thirty times. Dodging astutely, the gull splashes into the shallows. It may take off at once in the oppo-site direction or kick up water and refuse to fly up until the attack-ers have left.

There is no question that some peregrines can be deadly serious about gulls. Such a specialist occasionally visits the lake and demon-strates how it is done. Approaching head-on or from the side, it swoops up at a gull from below and makes only a single pass. The tar-get either flops aside gracelessly or is seized at once. Others are taken by complete surprise. One adult falcon snatched a Franklin's gull out of a flock that flushed in a panic from the water's edge. An immature, capitalizing on the element of surprise in quite a different way, climbed directly toward a gull that was hovering against a strong wind over the shore, hawking for insects. Approaching from behind and below, in the gull's blind spot, this crafty immature grabbed his prey point-blank. The gull never saw what hit it!

Even the common tern, the most elegant and shiftiest of flyers, which has the audacity to overtake and mob the peregrine, occa-sionally succumbs to surprise. One day, an immature tiercel took off from a post and flew low and fast to a small nesting island just beyond a stand of bulrush. Skimming over the reeds, the tiercel slammed into a dense flock of terns that took flight in the very last instant. Carrying his white booty, long wings dangling, he returned to his post.

Peregrines in flight. All are females except the bird in the picture immediately above. Note the extremely slender wings of this adult tiercel, typical of those that nest in the boreal and tundra regions of Canada, and now in central Alberta.

Overleaf, pages 66-67:
A rare shot of a peregrine attacking wigeon.

Peregrine eggs come in a range of warm browns and are somewhat larger than medium-sized chicken eggs. Barring accidents, they hatch after thirty-two to thirty-five days of incubation. In another six weeks or so, the chicks develop into fledglings, almost ready to go.

Overleaf, pages 72-73:
Female peregrine attending its chicks on a cliff eyrie in northern Canada.

Marsh ragwort and bulrushes, growing along the shores of Alberta's Beaverhills Lake, allow peregrines to hunt shore-birds by a strategy of stealth designed to surprise them at close range. *Photo: Dick Dekker*

Common prey species such as lesser yellowlegs, dowitchers and pectoral sandpipers. *Photo: Dick Dekker*

Over the open prairie pastures bordering the lake, waterfowl become vulnerable to attack when they fly from one body of water to the next.

Photo: Dick Dekker

Below: Even the tiny semi-palmated sandpiper is often captured.

Overleaf, pages 76-77: Migrating peregrines, such as this immature, that stop over at the lake do not mind to sit low on the ground, especially during high winds.

After a thirty-year absence, peregrines returned to breed on the Red Deer River in central Alberta, the successful result of mass releases of captive-raised young.

Above: A second-year bird, just back from migration, lays claim to the nest box on the cliff where it was hacked out in 1996. Resident prairie falcons compete with the peregrines for eyrie sites on natural cliff ledges.

Top left: The location where both species attempted to nest in 1998, as detailed in the epilogue.

Left: The young falconer is Sarah Trefry, daughter of Phil and Helen Trefry, who ran the Canadian Wildlife Service falcon breeding facility at Wainwright, Alberta. Over its twenty-five years of operation, the center produced 1752 young peregrines for release throughout Canada.

Localities in coastal British Columbia where the author conducted intensive studies of peregrine falcons.

Top left: In this agricultural valley on Vancouver Island, wintering falcons launched duck hunts from tall tree perches.

Below left: Over the intertidal flats at Boundary Bay, peregrines made spectacular, long-range attacks on massing sandpipers. Prominently visible on this clear afternoon is Mount Baker, Washington, fifty miles (80 km) away.

Above right: A cliff-top view of the Pacific Ocean at Langara Island in the Queen Charlottes. In this bay, Peale's falcons specialized on seabirds and were forced to cope with their ubiquitous enemy, the bald eagle.

Below: The rugged coast of Langara features deeply incised cliffs where nesting falcons find shelter from stormy weather.   *Photos: Dick Dekker*

Above: This ancient murrelet, cached on a nesting cliff at Langara, was found by Dr. Wayne Nelson, who has monitored the island's breeding population of marine peregrines since the late sixties.

If a peregrine kills a large or medium-sized bird, it typically does not pluck the wings, leaving them attached to the skeleton.
Left: An American wigeon.
Below: A Franklin's gull.   *Photos: Dick Dekker*

Peregrines love to hunt teal which are light enough to be carried out of reach of powerful pirates such as the bald eagle.

Left: A buffy-colored chest is generally diagnostic for the *anatum* subspecies, while northern peregrines have immaculate white chests. In the large Peale's peregrines of the northwest Pacific Coast the white chest is marked more or less heavily with streaking. Captive breeding programs, mixing stock from different origins, have produced birds of a range of plumages and sizes. However, a peregrine is a peregrine is a peregrine. Wild populations typically show much individual variation.

The big city has proven to be an attractive environment for peregrines ever since their strong return after the pesticide era. As of 1998, there are pairs nesting in sixty-six metropolitan centers across North America. Western Canadian cities were first colonized in 1980. Edmonton is home to three or four pairs that fiercely compete for suitable sites. They are monitored yearly by government personnel.

Above: Shown here is David Moore of Alberta Environmental Protection. Banding young can be made all the more challenging by the fierce attacks of enraged adults.

Upper right: While the majority of peregrines nesting in urban centers are the progeny of captive-raised stock, unbanded birds from unknown origin have shown up as well.

Lower right: A black-banded city falcon, herself the offspring of captive-bred parents, raises the next generation on a ledge of an Edmonton highrise.

The power generating stations by Wabamun Lake in central Alberta have become a hot spot for breeding peregrines soon after nest boxes were attached to the tall chimneys by the Alberta Falconers' Association with the cooperation of the plant's management.

Right: An adult male watches defiantly from the top railing of a smoke stack, while researchers are fitting his young with black leg bands. As indicated by his numbered red band, this tiercel was captive-raised and released in Winnipeg, over 800 miles (1200 km) to the east. Note his extremely slender profile and immaculate white chest. A very similar adult male at another Wabamun plant turned out to be the most fantastic hunter the author has watched anywhere!

Opposite page: Where the two species share living space, the bald eagle is the peregrine's nemesis, robbing the falcon of its prey. Near the nest site, its most dangerous antagonists are the goshawk and the great-horned owl.

While peregrines are quick to take food from the merlin *(above)*, and may even hunt this small falcon down as potential prey itself, they in turn are occasionally robbed by the prairie falcon *(below right)* and the gyr *(below left)*. Locally, these three large falcons also compete for cliff nesting sites. .

The nesting ecology of peregrines on the arctic coast of Keewatin has been studied by Gordon Court and his colleagues since 1980. They found that these falcons often feed their young on the nestlings of open-country passerines, as well as on lemmings and young arctic ground squirrels. During summers when these prolific rodents reach a cyclic population peak, the number of successful peregrine nests increases sharply and productivity soars.

Overleaf, pages 92-93: On guard near her nesting cliff. Immediately after spring arrival, by the middle of May, tundra falcons establish territories that are fiercely defended. Males as well as females engage in violent combat with intruders, sometimes leading to lethal results.

Overleaf, page 96: While peregrines routinely specialize in certain prey groups, such as waterfowl, seabirds, pigeons or passerines, other species, such as the flicker, are taken opportunistically when they pass over open country.

Survival of the swiftest

Those who take a passionate interest in the age-old spectacle between predator and prey tend to think that this bloody business makes sense in the way of selective effect. If we believe in the basic principles of natural selection, we want to find confirmation of this ideal in the rare moments when we are witnesses to the kill. Evidence to support our cherished notion seems lacking if a predator ruthlessly exploits the circumstances to pick its victim at random out of the milling crowd, such as the hovering gull and the nesting tern.

By contrast, positive evidence for selective effect seems obvious if we watch a prolonged pursuit in which both predator and prey appear to have a fair chance. The outcome should favor the fit over the weak, a concept that is a cornerstone of popular evolution theory. But how exactly does this work? Did the falcon recognize the prey's weakness from the start and did it therefore concentrate its effort on this particular individual? Or was the predator very hungry and willing to do its utmost to overcome even the fittest of prey? Does hunger motivate a falcon to be persistent in pursuit? Conversely, does a perceived lack of ardor indicate that a falcon is just playing? These same questions have been raised many times before. Some authors of handbooks think that falcons surely must be fooling around if they fail in more than four or five tries. After decades of observation in the field, I find the question more perplexing than ever. The difference between serious and not so serious hunts is often impossible to determine. From the start I too was puzzled by the fact that falcons often made just a single pass and gave up, whereas in other attacks they showed great determination. After more than 2,000 observations, I have to conclude that some hunts are indeed not serious, at their best just a test. However, if the prey fails to react in the right way it may be killed regardless. A scaup duck and a coot which made absolutely no attempt at dodging were caught and abandoned, just left in the grass. Evidently, these falcons were not in the mood to eat, yet they had killed. On the other hand, falcons which I knew to be hungry because they captured and consumed a prey immediately afterwards, might seem equally casual in their approach. Not looking too serious at all, at least to me, they selected their target with deliberate and lethal accuracy, spending no more energy than needed to make their kill.

No doubt peregrines know what they are doing. They have the ability to quickly appraise the strength and vigor of other birds. We do not have such acute powers of observation. Only in the most blatant instances can we recognize a disadvantaged bird, such as a crow with ragged wings laboring to make headway against the wind. A German falconer once published a list of data to show that his peregrine, trained to take crows, captured a relatively high percentage of individuals with physical defects compared to a control group of crows collected with a shotgun. The assumption was that the falcon selected some crows because they were cripples. Other observers have noted that peregrines take the odd one out, the only white pigeon in a dark flock, or the only dark one in a light-colored bunch. This seems to support the theory of selective effect. Predators weed out the unfit and aberrant among their prey and they probably get better at this task with experience.

Selective effect may even be at work in surprise attacks, not in favor of the prey but on the peregrine's side. Any kill is the falcon's gain. It has often struck me how accomplished adults are at using surprise. Taking their time, they plan their strategy and go in for the easy capture. Individual falcons that have refined such techniques maximize their chances for survival and procreation.

98

Chapter 7

The Duck Hawk in Action

For the migrating peregrine, passing over the interior plains of North America, there is a watershed of difference between its two major prey groups, shorebirds and ducks. Whereas the former can only find safety in flight, leaving them open to pursuit anytime, the latter are practically untouchable in their fluid element. But there is one major consolation: compared to teeny-weeny appetizers such as a sandpiper, even the smallest species of waterfowl provide a complete meal. Peregrines love to eat teal, wigeon, shoveler, pintail, scaup and gadwall. These can be as vulnerable as the proverbial sitting duck, but only on land....

One day many years ago, before I had seen any successful duck hunts at the lake, an immature falcon took off from a fence post by the shore. Long wings flicking smartly, it climbed steadily and menacingly, sharply outlined against an overcast sky over inland fields. Suddenly, a flock of ducks entered my field of view, approaching from the west, still far off. My mouth fell open and my heart began pounding in anticipation. The ducks recognized their enemy for they changed direction. The peregrine bore down on them fast. The last bird in the straggling line seemed doomed. Just as the falcon closed in, the duck dropped like a stone. The plunge was so narrowly timed that it looked as if the duck had been knocked out of the sky. In fact, it had splashed down into some floodwater to save its hide in the nick of time. During the first few years of observation I saw such evasive maneuvers so often that it seemed as if the falcons always failed. Yet, I found their kills on the pastures and along the shore.

The leftovers of a peregrine's meal can be recognized as such by the way the falcon feeds. Of the larger ducks, such as the pintail, most of the meat might have been removed, but the wings are not plucked and remain attached to the skeleton. Of the smaller species, such as teal, the head is usually cut off and abandoned. The chest bone shows triangular nicks left by the falcon's powerful bill. Finding their kills raised my hopes that one day I would be in the right spot at the right time. Assuming that most foraging activity took place in early morning, I spent many chilly hours watching perched falcons, keeping them in the glasses or telescope. To break the boredom, it was tempting to approach for a more detailed look. But that proved to be a tactical mistake. Moving up in slow stages, I would eventually get too close so the bird became uneasy and left. It was equally disappointing to find that some falcons had already made a kill, perhaps earlier in the morning, because they flew down to the grass nearby and began feeding. Checking the spot, I found the remains of ducks that seemed at least several hours old. Perhaps they had even been killed the previous night. Anyway, it was unlikely that the falcon would hunt again soon.

Seizing the moment

The long wait to see a successful duck hunt made me all the more appreciate the first kill, which turned into an odd surprise. It happened in late morning, soon after I arrived at the lake, delayed by rain. Far away, an adult falcon took off from its post and headed for a bird (a duck I thought) flying low over a pasture separating an inland slough from the main lake. Overtaking it rapidly, the peregrine seized its prey directly and dropped down out of sight. I was jumping for joy!

Approaching in slow stages, stopping frequently to scan the terrain through binoculars, I presently discovered the falcon standing in the sedges by the water's edge. It was not doing much and after a few minutes it flew away. Puzzled, I walked up and found a freshly killed coot! Equally surprising was the fact that not a single feather had been plucked. It seemed unlikely that the falcon had been scared off by my approach. Perhaps it had not been hungry enough, or may be it did not like the taste of coot? At any rate, it had obviously not resisted this easy catch. Coots, like other rails, are weak on the wing and slow to turn, a tempting target for any falcon.

Some time later I saw a similar incident when an adult female took off from a post and intercepted a pair of lesser scaup flying along the lake. The falcon seized and killed the drake but left him otherwise untouched in the grass. In this case, there was absolutely no possibility that I could have disturbed the falcon, for I had stayed where I was until she returned to her post. After a brief examination, I put the carcass back on the ground. The next day it had been mostly consumed, perhaps by the same falcon or by scavenging hawks.

The deadpan scenario of the above two examples proved to be typical of many other hunts. Catching ducks looked like the easiest thing in the world. Approaching directly, either from the side, from behind or even the front, the peregrine just grabbed its prey which made no attempt at dodging. Perhaps some ducks had not seen the falcon? Or were they just too slow to react? Several falcons that seized large ducks flying over marshes dropped them again, unable to carry them to land. Their prey plummeted into the reeds as if dead, but it was probably just stunned temporarily. Released at a moderate height over the lake, one duck fell a few feet and resumed flight!

Sitting ducks

The earliest migrant peregrines to arrive at Beaverhills show up in mid-April when much of the lake can still be frozen. The scarcity of open water makes flying ducks all the more vulnerable. The falcons hunt far out over the ice as well as along the thawing shallows along shore. An adult female pursued a scaup drake that had no place to go and splashed down in a puddle of meltwater, not deep enough to submerge. The falcon just landed on her prey and dragged it onto the edge of the ice.

After the lake has opened up, ducks are much safer, at least for a while. Like all prey species, their daily routine is governed by the often conflicting demands for food and security. From time to time, they haul out onto the edge of the ice or the shore to rest and preen for hours while some of them keep an eye peeled for danger. If large gatherings have been socializing peacefully for hours, you can be sure that no falcon has shown up for some time. On the other hand,

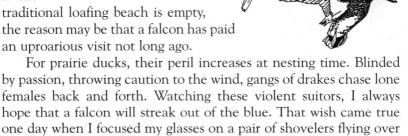

if the
traditional loafing beach is empty,
the reason may be that a falcon has paid
an uproarious visit not long ago.

For prairie ducks, their peril increases at nesting time. Blinded
by passion, throwing caution to the wind, gangs of drakes chase lone
females back and forth. Watching these violent suitors, I always
hope that a falcon will streak out of the blue. That wish came true
one day when I focused my glasses on a pair of shovelers flying over
golden stubble, one of the prettiest sights of spring in Alberta.
Suddenly a peregrine, white and blue as the sky above, entered the
picture and grabbed the drake, bearing him down onto the field.

During egg-laying time, instead of hiding their affairs under the
cloak of darkness, some mated pairs of ducks fly to the land in early
evening. Scurrying about in the grass, they are at the mercy of peregrines passing overhead on their northward migration or sitting on a
post not far away. One of the pair may be nailed down before it has
time to get off the ground. Ducks feeding or dozing in open terrain
are always at risk. If the prey flushes and dodges the first strike by
dropping back onto the ground, perhaps strafed by talons, the falcon
turns and grabs its victim without hesitation. Wings flapping for balance, it shifts its grip to the neck and inserts its bill between the vertebrae, delivering the *coup de grace*. Yet, it may take from five to ten
minutes before the struggle ends. After looking in all directions,
checking for pirates, the falcon begins to feed, pulling out gobs of
feathers and strewing them all around. It first eats the fatty skin of
the neck, then the top of the breast. About half an hour later, stuff-
ing itself hurriedly, the falcon is ready to resume its journey, top-
heavy with a bulging crop. Or it may perch nearby and rest, perhaps
staying the night, to return to its kill at daybreak.

Grabbing a bite

Some duck hawks do not seem particular as to where they bring down their prey, on dry land, in mud, shallow water or tall grass, even between bushes. One wet and windy May evening, I was standing in the lee of some willows, when an immature falcon flew by along the reedy shore at an altitude of about fifty feet (15 m). Far away, several dozen ducks flushed out of a marshy corner and headed for the lake. The last to rise was cut off from its escape route. It turned back and descended steeply. Unhurried, the falcon went down on the same spot. Keeping my glasses trained on the area for several minutes, I did not see her rise again, so I decided to investigate.

Locating a kill is always more difficult than it seems. From a distance it may look simple, but once you get close to the area your search can take much longer than anticipated. As always, I carefully lined up some bearings, a distant fence post, as a rough guide for direction. Once I had entered the marsh, I expected the falcon to flush, betraying the exact location of her kill. However, when I got there, I was not sure anymore which post was my bearing, and the water became deeper with every step. Moreover, there was no sign of the falcon. Had she taken off unseen? Refusing to give up so easily, I went back to the willows and lined up my sights again, carefully counting the fence posts. A couple of crows passing over the marsh circled low and cawed excitedly, an indication that the falcon should still be there. I finally flushed her out of knee-high grasses. Her kill was a gadwall duck, submerged in water, belly down. The top of its back had been plucked and a little meat taken. After my departure, the falcon returned and flew over the marsh as if to check on her kill. But instead of landing, she left again and went out of sight to the north. Easy come, easy go....

An example of obvious waste such as the above might shock those who have placed the peregrine on a pedestal, but we must remember that this exalted creature, despite its grand reputation, is no better and no worse than other predators; if hungry, it kills whenever it can and in any way it can.

High in the sky

In contrast to the down to earth hunting methods described above, the duck hawk employs a host of other strategies more worthy of its high reputation. Soaring among the clouds, it does not hesitate to stoop at ducks flying below. These lofty attacks easily escape notice and may be more common than we know. One evening, at my approach, an adult peregrine left its post and climbed into the wind until it found a thermal. Far away, soaring high over the shore, it suddenly streaked down in a terrific stoop at a bird flying below. It could have been a pintail drake, but the distance involved was too great to be sure. The target veered aside and mounted steeply, the low sun gleaming on its white underside. Resuming its course, the bird gradually descended with the falcon hot on its tail until both disappeared from sight behind trees. A few days later I was back in the area and found the carcass of a pintail drake, all picked clean. Assuming that these were the remains of the bird I had seen chased, I felt bad to have missed the deciding stage of the hunt, especially since I had not seen any duck kills at all by that time. And another opportunity to witness a high-altitude attack did not materialize until much later. It proved to be equally frustrating.

This hunt took place right overhead while I was lying on my back in the grass, the glasses trained on a soaring adult female peregrine. Between spells of circling high in the blue sky, she twice stooped at pintails passing below her. One of them reacted in the same way as the bird in the first observation, shifting aside and abruptly rising after the stoop. Another drake, upon being attacked, plummeted down as fast as the falcon could stoop. Giving up on both, the falcon resumed her soaring pitch, no doubt ready for the next assault. Unfortunately, I had to take my eyes off her because in the meantime I had been surrounded by a herd of snorting, stomping cattle. After I had shooed them away, I was unable to relocate the falcon!

My big day finally arrived one May evening when an immature falcon took to the sky, soaring up to a great height. She suddenly stopped circling and launched a tremendous assault, wings flicking close to the tail. Far away I saw her target, a string of approaching ducks! Met head-on by the peregrine, the outermost bird dropped like a stone. The falcon stooped after it, but just before it was over-taken the duck twisted aside, zigzagging back and forth. Following closely, the falcon succeeded in grabbing her shifty prey. Still very high in the sky, wings set, she planed down far inland. Despite searching for more than an hour, I was unable to locate the falcon. Judging by size, her prey could have been a teal or a lesser scaup.

In subsequent years, I saw other soaring falcons stoop at flying ducks. If they succeeded in grabbing hold of their prey, it looked like the simplest thing in the world. The ducks neither dodged nor strug-gled. Seized from behind, they hang limp in the falcon's feet and were carried down to the ground. As of this writing, I have chalked up a combined total of seventy-eight captures of ducks, in Alberta and elsewhere. As stated earlier, only one of these involved an aeri-al hit. A teal, attacked from ahead and below, fluttered to the ground as if crippled by a shotgun blast, while the falcon turned about and calmly descended on her quarry.

Deliberate and deadly

Adult peregrines, like all birds of prey, are great strategists. In the open terrain around Beaverhills, they like to perch on posts between the lake and inland wetlands where ducks frequently cross from one body of water to the other. Intercepting its prey, the falcon flies very low, often meeting the duck head-on and swooping steeply upward with reaching claws. These attacks are deliberate and deadly, pre-venting the duck's usual plunging escape tactics. However, if few birds are flying and short-range hunts remain unproductive, the fal-cons switch to active search flight. Some stay low, hugging the ground over long distances. Others climb steadily to a cruising alti-tude of more than 300 feet (100 m). Watching them disappear, fol-lowing the shore or heading out over inland fields, I fervently wished I could fly with them! The closer my point of observation had been to its perch, the quicker the falcon vanished from sight, descending to attack far away. So I decided to keep my distance. With luck the falcon might come in my direction and I would end up much closer to the terminal stage of the hunt.

Predictably, most falcons went the other way, but one evening my luck changed. An adult female had made an aborted pass at ducks over the shore and returned to her post. She was obviously in a hunting mood and her appetite would grow as the evening progressed. In stop-and-go fashion, each time taking a quick look to check if she was still there, I increased the distance between us. When she was no more than a tiny speck against the skyline, I found a stone to sit on and aimed the glasses, just in time to see her take off. After reaching the lake shore, she did not go back to her post, but instead continued to climb out over the wide bay separating us. It was a thrilling sight to see her approach! She passed over with the deceptively casual wingbeat that I knew so well of falcons that are deadly serious. Having come from a mile away, she should be ready for the attack at any time and I held my breath. But she kept on going, decreasing in size again. When she was reduced to a flickering speck against the red western sky, she abruptly changed course and began to descend. She had sighted prey! Beating her wings furiously, she accelerated and curved down into a blistering stoop. Below her, just beyond a fence line dividing the crest of a sloping field, a pair of ducks was hurrying toward the lake. The falcon slammed down, out of sight, and only one duck flew on.

Some fifteen minutes later, breathlessly scanning the ploughland on the other side of the barbed wire fence, I caught sight of her standing in the furrows. Keen on learning what she had killed, I approached. She protested in a belligerent cackle, flying up to meet me. I am sure she would have driven me off with a blow to the head if only she had dared to approach my dreaded human shape! Instead, circling back, she retreated and landed some distance away. The prey turned out to be a female mallard, her bloody breast cradled in a bed of down. The eyes were open and still as clear as in life. She must have looked her killer straight in the masked face, seen the toothed beak coming down....

Night hunting

There is another characteristic and deadly duck hunting strategy that I discovered quite by coincidence. Curious to find out where peregrines go for the night, I continued to watch a perched immature female that had not moved since early evening. At dusk, I was satisfied that she would stay put. But just after I turned away to start the long walk back to the road, the falcon flew by low over the pasture. Following her in the glasses, I saw her swoop up at a couple of ducks which dodged out of harm's way. The falcon returned a little later, going the other way. Just before fading from view in the gathering darkness, she made another pass at a pair of ducks, again failing to connect.

Since then, I learned that some of these passage birds indeed spend the hours of darkness sitting on fence posts in the open. They especially like a roost over water, where they probably feel safest from owls or mammalian predators. However, I also saw more evidence of night hunting activity. One bird left her post so late that she became lost to view as soon as she became airborne. On other evenings, well after sundown, alerted by the chorus of angry blackbirds, I spotted falcons hunting low over the reedy shore.

From the peregrine's point of view, night hunting makes sense; it maximizes the element of surprise. Ducks are very active after dusk and clearly visible against the light sky while the hunter is hidden low over the dark fields. Peregrines do not mind eating at night. Captive birds are commonly fed while hooded and unable to see. The falcon's luminous eyes do well by the stars. Its hunger stilled, the duck hawk returns to a post, perhaps the one it had selected before the hunt, to roost until morning. At first light, it may go back to the carcass for another meal.

One bright evening after sunset, while ducks began rising from the lake to resume their migration, an immature female climbed high over the northwest bay. Vainly trying to soar in the cooling night air, she flew in circles, winging back and forth as if climbing a stair case. Suddenly, she stooped at a small flock of ducks passing below her. She seized one of them and descended steeply onto the stubble field. Anxious to find her kill before dark, I hurried to the spot, flushing the falcon. Her prey was a lesser scaup. Retreating at once, I hoped that she would return soon but she did not. Driving my station wagon onto the adjacent pasture, I spent the night and rose at the crack of dawn. Training the telescope on the spot where I had found the dead scaup, I saw a slight movement in the stubble: the falcon's head bobbing up and down. She had returned to last night's kill! I felt more than pleased and relieved after disturbing her so rudely last night. I now understood why my earlier attempts at seeing falcons hunt in early morning had been so frustrating. Not only did peregrines stay active in the evening longer than humans, they also got up much earlier!

Enemies and scavengers

There is one additional reason why night hunting makes sense for peregrines. As daylight fades, the risk of losing prey to larger raptors should decline. Falcons are especially vulnerable to piracy if they have caught a duck that is too heavy to be carried out of reach of thieves. On the West Coast, the bald eagle is an omnipresent bully. But at Beaverhills Lake, most eagles have already passed through by the time spring migration of peregrines begins. Then, the main adversaries are buteos. Only big female falcons have the clout to discourage a determined red-tailed hawk. Tiercels do not even try. One evening I watched an immature male catch two teal in five minutes. He lost the first one to a red-tail, the second to a Swainson's hawk. Without any attempt at defense, the tiercel flew to a nearby post and sat there until sundown. He then left on determined wings while dusk shrouded the fields and the buteos were retiring for the night.

Yet, not all red-tails appear to be eager to rob a falcon. Perhaps it depends on the state of their appetite and their food preference. Subsisting mainly on rodents, which can be torn up and swallowed easily, some red-tails may not even like a thickly feathered duck unless it is properly prepared. This notion came to mind after an intriguing sequence of observations, one evening in mid-April, when several dozen ducks were gathering on a lakeside stubble field. Always thinking peregrine, I was hoping that the first falcon of the season might show up before it was time for the hour-long drive back to the city. Scanning the field, brightly lit by the low sun, I noticed that a flock of Canada geese was all looking in the same direction. Following their gaze in the binoculars, I discovered an adult peregrine on the ground, flapping its wings and struggling mightily. He looked small enough to be a tiercel and he had obviously just caught a large prey. Quickly setting up the scope, I saw that it was a pintail drake. A minute or so later, the tiercel abruptly abandoned his catch and flew to a fence post some hundred yards away. The reason was clear; a big, female red-tailed hawk, mantling in the stubble, had taken over his prey! But she soon departed. Leaving the prey behind, she flew to the same fence line the peregrine was sitting on. This seemed very odd behavior indeed.

The poor drake was still on the spot, poking his head up out of the stubble and looking about. Wounded, he was probably unable to flee. His suffering ended a few minutes later, when he was again grabbed by the tiercel. This time, the struggle was over quickly and the peregrine began to pluck, but not for long. Once more he was routed by the red-tail. The hawk now found the food better to her liking and fed without interruption. Presently she was joined by her mate, which waited for his turn at the table. Before both flew away to the woods, several harriers arrived and moved up for a share of the spoils. By now the sun had dropped below the horizon and the tiercel was still on his post. Once or twice, he had flown by the hawks as if to check on the leftovers. Each time he had gone back to a perch, biding his time. Perhaps he was waiting for dusk. But I had to get back home and unlike peregrines I do not like traveling in the dark.

Veterans and novices

In stark contrast to the spring passage, the return movement of peregrines at the lake is hardly noteworthy. The first falcons may show up in late August, but I have yet to see one after 5 October. And even though I visit the lake at least twice a week every fall, the total number of sightings is seldom more than two or three per season. Southbound Arctic migrants may choose a different route than in spring, perhaps more easterly. This was born out in 1997 when scientists Mark Bradley and Geoffry Holroyd captured an adult female peregrine, nesting in northern Alberta, and fitted her with a satellite transmitter. By late August, she was already on her way south, traveling in a straight line through Saskatchewan and the Dakotas to the Texas Gulf coast. It covered between 200 and 400 miles (320–640 km) per day. On 11 September she had already reached her wintering grounds south of Veracruz, Mexico!

Similarly, there is a vast seasonal difference in shorebird migrations at the lake. Instead of the concentrated passage of spring, returning migrants are spread over a wider time slot and perhaps also a wider front. By early July, barely three weeks after the last of the northbound stragglers have gone by, the vanguard is on the way back. Local concentrations may occur from late July into early September, dependent upon several factors such as the extent of mudflat habitat. In general, the vast majority of shorebirds has passed through before I see the first falcons.

During fall I spend most of my time along the southeast shore of the lake, the opposite side as in spring. If a fair number of shorebirds, perhaps several hundred, have gathered in the shallows of the southeast bay, I like to sit quietly on a vantage point nearby, especially on the first clear day after a prolonged rainy spell. With luck, I may pick up a peregrine that approaches along the straight east shore and launches an attack in the bay. Pragmatic and experienced, adults waste a minimum of time on foraging. After the hunt, they continue their southward journey at once.

One early morning I found an adult female perched on a post by the south shore. Two hours later, after the day had warmed, she took off, going west, climbing steadily and following the lake. I am sure she knew exactly, as I did, where all the ducks were: at a bait site where government personnel had deposited grain so as to lure hungry fowl away from unharvested farm crops. Nearing the bait station, the falcon slanted down in a high speed attack. Following her in the glasses, I saw hundreds of ducks rise in alarm. She swooped low among them, came back up for a moment and descended hurriedly into the grass. Walking to the area, about a mile away, I discovered her standing on the marshy shore, screened by rushes. Her movements indicated she was feeding. Careful not to disturb her, I kept my distance until she left, top-heavy with a distended crop. She rested briefly on a post, cleaning her bill on the wood. Then she climbed into the breeze and soared away to the south, resuming migration. Her prey, lying in shallow water, was a female pintail. Only the neck and part of the breast had been consumed. One hunt, one kill!

Juvenile spunk

The hunting success rate of fall immatures is quite another matter and tricky to determine. Young peregrines are active and fun to watch, fooling around with other hawks, robbing merlins of prey, harassing ducks in the shallows and chasing prey hither and thither. But it is not always clear what qualifies as a bonafide hunt and what is just play. For this reason I collected my data conservatively, and the total number of hunts grew very slowly. After thirty-three years of watching at the lake I have recorded about 100 hunts by fall immatures. Successful ones were so rare that I can clearly remember all seven of them.

There is a big difference in style between juvenile males and females. Some tiercels already hunt much in the same way as adults. Flying high, they barrel down to the shore at terrific speed, flushing shorebirds in a perfect attempt at surprise. I saw them seize two flee-ing sandpipers from behind and carry them along low over the shal-lows. Unfortunately for him, one of the juvenile males was at once robbed by a larger falcon.

In contrast to the stylish little tiercels, females bully their way to a meal. Apart from stealing from their brothers, they chase prey with brutal directness, driving it down to the ground. Several long pur-suits of gulls and black-bellied plovers went clear out of sight. In Saskatchewan, over open terrain, J. B. Rose followed a hunt by car and reported that an immature falcon chased and repeatedly swooped at a Franklin's gull for a distance of at least four miles (6 km) before it was caught.

During evening, young females cruise over the reedy shore of the lake in low search flight. Dashing into openings, they fall upon ducks, coots or sandpipers without warning. Twice I saw a lesser yellowlegs succumb to their guerilla tactics. Protesting loudly, the desperate shorebird evaded the falcon's clumsy passes by dropping into the shal-lows and flying up at once again. After succeeding twenty or thirty times, the yellowlegs finally made a fatal mistake by jumping up at the wrong moment, right into the clutches of the swooping falcon.

Lacking style and finesse, young peregrines compensate with stamina and perseverance. They have the innate ability to chase down prey in any open landscape, yet they need all the luck in the world to survive their first hazardous journey south. Those that return north in spring are veterans of a thousand hunts.

Chapter 8

Pacific Island Intrigue

Nearly one mile away, perched on the bare snag of the tallest conifer protruding above the rugged coastline, the peregrine looks tiny but clearly visible against the sky. Through the twenty-power, wide-angle telescope I can see his white breast gleaming in the sun. He is the male of the resident pair and he is "still-hunting." This morning he has already made several flights, heading out over the ocean at great speed and descending low over the water. But every time he has returned to his high perch without prey, leaving me wondering as to his intentions. Following his flight path in the scope, I had seen no birds that could possibly have been his target, either fleeing or splashing down in the nick of time.

From my observation point on a 100-foot (30 m) cliff I could overlook a wide bay, dotted with small alcids (a family of diving birds), mostly murrelets and auklets. Others flew singly or in groups very low over the surface. These saltwater divers are known to be the major prey of the peregrines that breed here on Langara Island, the most northerly outlier of the mountainous Queen Charlotte chain called *Haida Gwaii* by the Native tribes. The remains of small alcids, particularly the ancient murrelet, are much in evidence on nest ledges of the Langara peregrines which have been monitored for thirty years by Wayne Nelson and, before him, by Frank Beebe. As Frank described it, the murrelet is a compact little sea bird with "the body of a pigeon and the wings of a swallow." Its straight, unbending flight makes it an easy prey for peregrines...if they can catch it in the air!

Spending most of their life on the ocean, feeding on shrimplike krill or zooplankton, the murrelets do not fly much. However, during spring and early summer they commute to and from their nests on the island. In the mossy forest floor, at the end of a burrow, the female lays two eggs, which are relatively large, giving the well-developed, precocious chicks a head start in life. Soon after hatching, they have to find their way back to the ocean on their own, clambering over tree roots and rocks, traversing steep slopes and densely treed ravines. After they get through the pounding surf, the lucky ones, guided by calls, reunite with their parents. It is a miracle of irrepressible life forces and blind faith in survival that has been going on for millennia.

During the incubation stage, the adult murrelets take turns brooding, relieving each other under the cloak of darkness every few days. At the crack of dawn, just when the departing bird flies over the wave-washed shore, the tiercel, hunting for his mate and brood, drops eagerly off a high snag. A few seconds later, the prey hangs limply in his talons. Death for one, life for the other, a routine transaction along these wilderness shores, yet rarely witnessed by humans. By chance, half a dozen of these straightforward, early morning kills had been observed by government biologists doing research in murrelet nesting colonies. However, very little was known about the hunting habits of these marine peregrines outside the breeding season. This is what I had come to investigate, in my own time, driven by pure curiosity about this species. Now, in late August, the murrelets were enjoying the best of times. The ocean abounded in food. In another month or so, the raging winter storms would start. By that time, the young should have learned an essential lesson—how to cope with their enemies.

The scope glued to my eye, I am waiting for the tiercel to launch his next foray. For the past half hour he has not moved, but not for a second do I let him out of my sight. Nothing is so annoying as losing a falcon because of a moment of inattentiveness after having watched it for a long and usually very dull amount of time. This morning I have been looking at this tiercel for close to four hours and the tension is building. It is a relief to again see the flicker of his spreading wings. As before, he heads out over the ocean. Holding my breath, I concentrate on turning the tripod ever so smoothly. As long as the peregrine is black against the sky, keeping him in focus is easy enough, but it becomes very tricky once he descends low over the sea, increasing his speed. His rapid wingbeats become shallower, then he glides, the merest speck of gray dissolving over a gray ocean. Damn! With a pang of disappointment, I let go of the scope and grab my binoculars to scan the skyline. When I find the tiercel again, he is already heading back to his perch. Lowering the glasses, I refocus the scope and prepare for another wait.

Mercifully, this time he leaves soon. He must be getting hungry! And to my delight he chooses a direction bringing him closer instead of carrying him farther away. After his descent low over the kelp-infested shore, I can keep the scope very still, the falcon in the center growing in size, a white dot over the smooth bay. Setting his wings, he skims over the surface and suddenly I notice there is a murrelet on the water directly in his line of flight. In the next split-second, it dives with a splash, inches in front of its attacker. The tiercel passes over the spot, pulls up and turns back to his perch. I am elated. My suspicions of this morning have been confirmed. The peregrine is indeed attacking swimming prey!

At the terminus of his next hunt, which begins in the same way as before, there is again a murrelet right in the peregrine's path. But this one is apparently unaware of the danger and too late to react. The tiercel dips slightly lower and connects, striking his prey. The next instant he shoots almost straight upward and just as quickly turns back down to seize the floundering murrelet, lifting it from the surface and carrying it away. This time, the tiercel does not return to his snag but disappears into a narrow ravine where he and his mate raised their young earlier in the season. He will eat his prize in the seclusion of a rocky cave, festooned with moss and ferns.

On subsequent days I see nine other captures much like the first, either by the male or the female, and twenty-nine unsuccessful attacks, all directed at swimming alcids. Because of the distance involved, not every hunt could be followed in complete detail. But its objective and outcome seemed plain if I saw a bird diving to dodge the attack, either well ahead or in the very last instant. Murrelets and auklets spread their wings to submerge. They actual-

114

ly fly under water! The slight splash of their dive can be seen from a considerable distance, especially in smooth water.

If the ocean was rough, the falcons used the swell to conceal their approach. Fellow observer Ludo Bogaert saw clearly that one alcid on the crest of a wave dived, but another in the trough of the next wave and also directly in line with the falcon's flight path was hit and retrieved. The pair also appeared to use a large, surf-washed boulder as cover, trying to surprise prey on the other side.

Twelve hunts were directed at birds in flight, ten of them in vain. Murrelets and other alcids never fly higher than a few feet above the ocean and as soon as they spot an approaching falcon they plunge straight down, hitting the water hard and diving at once. In one hunt, after leaving her perch on the high snag, the falcon streaked low over the waves and slammed into a flock of half a dozen alcids. She grabbed one of them at once while the others dived down in a fountain of spray. As she turned back to the island, a slight bulge under her tail betrayed that she was indeed carrying prey. This was also obvious to other eyes, keener than mine. Two eagles hurriedly flew to intercept the falcon, but she climbed hard and managed to stay out of their reach. Pursuit by eagles was another indicator that a falcon, returning from a distant hunt, had been successful. The pressure from these powerful pirates never lets up.

Ocean battle

All along the island's coast, sitting on snags and rocky headlands, eagles spied on other ocean birds. They were very well able to capture waterfowl if they set their mind to it, but they subsisted on fish, dead or alive, from the smallest to the biggest. Dozens might share a bonanza such as the carcass of a stranded whale. Others were content to pick up two-inch (5 cm) minnows, one by one. In Alberta, at spring break-up, I once saw migrating eagles feed on dead stickle-backs washed down by a creek onto the ice of Beaverhills Lake!

Here on Langara, the lazy giants used other birds as unwitting scouts. Patrolling the ocean, the glaucous-winged gulls were usually first to spot a floating cod or rockfish. Dozens of gulls, as well as shearwaters, auklets and cormorants, quickly collected if schools of sandlance boiled up from the depths and broke the surface in their panic to escape salmon or whales. In seconds, the feeding frenzy was joined by eagles circling the spot. Swooping down, they dragged their big feet and scooped up a fistful of tiny fishes. Consumed in flight, some were spilled and fell back into the water like slivers of silver. These scenes were a daily occurrence and always fun to watch. One time, just as two eagles descended eagerly, a humpback whale rose out of the water with gaping maw, swallowing most of the "boil" of sandlance. The eagles pulled up in the nick of time!

In spite of the ample food supply in this rich marine ecosystem, klepto-parasitism was second nature to the eagles. Pumping their great wings, they rushed near as soon as a peregrine had struck an alcid on the water. Starting from a high perch, they were surprisingly fast, leaving a falcon very little time to retrieve its wounded prey. This could be made even more difficult if the alcid, though crippled, was still capable of thrashing about, foiling the falcon's aim. If contact had not been achieved in three tries, the first of the approaching eagles secured the alcid in one smooth pass, never slowing down and keeping on going. Of course, old baldy is an expert at this game, whereas the peregrine has to execute the maneuver with precision, slowing down just enough against the breeze. Even after a timely retrieval, the falcon did not always get away scot-free. One morning, the female had great trouble evading a persistent pursuer that made pass after pass. With a loud swooshing of wings both birds swept by the cliff Ludo and I were standing on. Unable to gain enough altitude to rise over the steep shoreline, the falcon surrendered her prey which fell into a tangle of rocks and vegetation, lost to all.

It was abundantly clear that the eagle was an opponent to reckon with and difficult to avoid. The unrelenting threat of piracy might explain why the Langara falcons never preyed on the larger alcids such as the locally common pigeon guillemot. Weighing about one pound (450 g), this sea diver is well within range of the peregrine's capabilities. However, in all of his thirty years of nest research on Langara, Wayne Nelson never found guillemot remains on eyrie ledges. By contrast, the very similar black guillemot is a common prey for peregrines nesting on the treeless Arctic coast of Keewatin, where bald eagles are absent. At Langara it would be folly for peregrines to weigh themselves down with a bird the size of a guillemot.

They suffered enough eagle trouble as it was with a seven-ounce (200 g) murrelet!

These basic facts of life may have to be learned the hard way by the young. One warm afternoon, a large juvenile female, just independent and mercilessly chased away from shore by the adults, flew out over the ocean and began to soar. She suddenly flew down obliquely, raced low over the water and grabbed a fairly large bird, probably a guillemot or a similar-sized rhinoceros auklet. Carrying her bulky prey back to land, the falcon was hotly pursued by an adult eagle which easily kept up with the heavily laden peregrine and made one shallow swoop after the other. The falcon shifted aside each time, refusing to surrender her prey. The two disappeared from view behind a headland and I never learned whether this brazen but perhaps foolish youngster had managed to carry it off. ("Carrying it off" is perhaps another term derived from falconry origins!)

I tend to think that adult peregrines would be loath to run the gauntlet of an eagle in such a close contest. The risk of losing more than the prey and finding themselves in the clutches of their mighty adversary is real.

Falconers who fly captive-raised peregrines can tell many colorful stories about young birds. Some behave like babes in the woods, innocents in the dog-eat-dog world of wild competitors, although they learn quickly. One immature, after a brutal confrontation with a red-tail, refused to go up as long as one of these powerful hawks was in the air. Another juvenile peregrine, owned by a Dutch falconer, turned into a "buzzard-specialist." This slow-flying buteo might have looked like easy prey to her: "Here is a bird I can catch!" The falcon tackled one again on the day when I had been invited along. We ran as fast as we could to disengage the combatants struggling on the ground. Before we got there, the buzzard flew away, possibly unharmed, but the falcon was left a cripple. Later, one of her legs had to be amputated! No doubt, similar tragedies may strike wild birds.

Taking what is easiest to get away with, the Peale's peregrines of Langara frequently utilize sea birds even smaller than murrelets and auklets. Prey remains on nest ledges include the wings of storm petrels. These swallows of the sea only approach land during the night. Capturing them far out over the ocean, the falcon may bite off the long wings and discard them in flight. In his famous *Life Histories of North American Birds of Prey*, Arthur C. Bent quotes a 1858 report that a peregrine came aboard a sailing bark more than a hundred miles out from California. From his perch on the masthead, the falcon launched hunts at petrels, taking at least a dozen of "these unsuspecting wanderers of the deep" in two days. Since then there have been numerous other reports of peregrines far at sea. At Langara I saw falcons leave the coast at a fair height and disappear from sight. Others soared. Spotting prey, they stooped to low over the surface. After a failed attack, they did not always return to land but continued on, heading straight out over the ocean.

During August, a common migratory shorebird passing Langara is the phalarope. Seeking food, it floats on the water like a cork, twirling and turning. The tiercel hunted it the same as alcids, primarily in a stealth approach. Phalaropes that flushed in time were pursued briefly, others plucked from the surface. This is of course only feasible if the prey is light enough. I saw just one such incident whereby the tiercel snatched an alcid directly from the surface. This was possibly a Cassin's auklet, which is even smaller than the murrelet. During stormy and rainy days the falcons darted among the waves, hugging the contours like shearwaters, perhaps using the momentum of heaving swells to snatch prey from the crest.

It was, however, easy to imagine that this environment could be all the more challenging during the long winter when the island is battered by storm after storm or shrouded in fog. As reported by Wayne Nelson, the adults stay at Langara all year, occupying their eyrie site. However, we will never know how many falcons, hunting far out at sea, end up in a watery grave.

A portion of the peregrine population of the northwestern Pacific Coast, particularly nonterritorial adults and immatures, have the freedom to wander down to more southerly environs. How some of them fare on their wintering grounds is detailed in the next chapters.

Chapter 9

On Winter Fields

Sharply set against a gray winter sky, three falcons, like tiny black tridents, are swirling together, graceful but deceptively innocent. In sudden bursts of speed, they strafe each other with vicious stoops, wind shuddering by their furled pinions. Flapping furiously in close pursuit, they roll and tangle, grappling talons. Their belligerent cackling drifts down to the earthbound watcher far below.

The aerial battle is taking place high over the hilly coastline of Vancouver Island. Below, the land drops off steeply to a narrow beach, rimmed by ceaseless ocean surf. The misty horizon is studded with islands, like stranded whales. The vastness of sea and sky seems limitless, yet these falcons are fighting over a few wet fields and ponds just inland. There, ducks slobber aquatic crustaceans and plants, all part of the food chain that supplies the metabolic energy to sustain lofty predators. At the apex of this interdependent world, the soaring peregrine seems supreme, but it is governed by what it eats, shackled to the mud below. Among each other, the falcons compete ferociously for territory, for the right to rule the ducks.

After a few minutes, two of the combatants have drifted far downwind, and the victor, a large adult falcon, is on her way back. On set wings, she glides over her domain. Her brilliant eyes scan the tilting kaleidoscope of land and water far below. Turning her black-capped head, she looks down and scrutinizes me, standing in the lee of a barn. Fearless or indifferent, she passes directly overhead, her long wings rigid, the barrel-shaped body tapering to a narrow tail. Through the binoculars, I can see that her throat and breast are nearly pure white. Belly and flanks are barred with black. When she banks and wheels, spreading her tail, her gray back glints like steel.

Gradually, she begins to descend and gain speed, wings partly flexed. She falls steeply, then levels out close to the ground. Keeping her in my circular core of view, all else flashes by in a blur: skyline, woodlots, farm buildings, a road. Gulls rise in alarm from ploughland. Starlings bunch and rush into trees. Over floodwater, a dozen ducks hurry to safety. Overtaken in an instant, just when a strike seems imminent, the flock splays apart and splashes down. The falcon zooms up over them like a rising star.

On the water, the ducks are spared further attack. She hangs still for a moment, suspended on the breeze, then veers crosswind and returns to her favorite perch, a huge cottonwood that stands like a sentinel in the center of the fields. This tree was her starting point from where I had first watched her fly off to challenge and evict the intruders. Now, after she swoops up to alight on a bare branch, I can finally lower the binoculars and rest my aching arms. Behind the barn I find some scrap lumber to improvise a seat. Resting elbows on knees, I aim the glasses again and wait.

Against a dark background of forested hills that cradle the low-lying enclave of farmland, the falcon is barely visible, her chest a tiny speck of white. She may perch quietly for hours or fly off soon, perhaps to choose another vantage point or to leave the area. But with luck, I may see another thrilling hunt. Then, all tedium and hardship will be forgotten at once.

This waterlogged nook of Vancouver Island is far from a pristine landscape. It is under intensive cultivation for market gardening and hay production. During winter, after heavy rains, flooded depressions become a haven for dabbling ducks, which in turn attract peregrines. Wary but used to the sight of farm workers and birdwatchers, the falcons often perch on power poles along the road or on TV antennas and trees in farm yards. It proves that human habitation and exciting wildlife do not always have to be mutually exclusive and that the peregrine is a highly adaptable species. Unfortunately, in recent years drainage ditches and the building of more houses along the perimeter have led to a decline in the area's value as a refuge for waterfowl and hence for their predators. While the good times lasted, over a dozen winters, I spent many days here to observe the falcons, to see them hunt, to learn first-hand how they captured the ducks and how they got along, or did not get along, with the powerful and ubiquitous bald eagle.

The cottonwood queen

Surveying her territory from the big cottonwood, the adult female seemed to abide by a simple motto: take it easy. As far as that can be said of a falcon, compared to the active migrants on the Alberta plains, the cottonwood falcon led a sedentary life, set in her habits. If the wind was too strong, she preferred to sit on the ground, facing into the breeze. After a good meal, she might take a bath in a shallow pool, walking up to her belly in water and fluttering her wings like a gull. Retiring to her perch, she would do very little for the rest of the day except preen, fussing over every feather with infinite care. Only the sight of another female peregrine could arouse her from her contented lethargy. Aggressive defense flights happened almost daily, proof of the fact that there was no lack of contenders for her territory. Most of the time, intruding falcons passed over high, unless the cottonwood queen was not at home, which happened quite regularly. She could be gone for part of the day or for several days in a row. As far as I knew, she had at least one alternate hunting ground on the other side of the wooded ridge that separated this enclave from the next wetland, a short distance inland. In her absence, the local ducks enjoyed a much-needed rest, which was important; if she harassed them too often, they might desert the place.

The cottonwood queen always left in the evening, just after sundown, probably moving to a roosting site. Not far away, on the Skagit Flats just south of the Canadian border, wintering falcons had been captured and fitted with transmitters. These birds also departed their farmland hunting grounds by evening and apparently flew to roosts on offshore cliffs. I never found out where the cottonwood queen spent the night, but I was always happy to see her back in the morning.

Upon arrival, around first light, I scanned her favorite perches. If there was no sign of her I would go for a walk, actually relieved that I was not at once compelled to watch her, which could have meant hours of inactivity. One pleasant morning, soon after I had parked the car and started a stroll around the fields, my approach caused numerous ducks to flush from the edge of floodwater. Following them in the glasses, I picked up the falcon in hot pursuit! In no time at all, she seized and released two ducks in quick succession. Each time the capture happened over water and she was forced to let go again, unable to carry her prey to dry land. Evidently, earlier this morning, when I could not find the falcon and had entered the fields, she had been watching me instead!

Hoping for a repeat of the above experience, I stuck to the same routine on other days when the falcon was not in sight. I tried to lure her by putting up ducks from the ponds, ditches and flooded fields. One morning when a pintail flushed just ahead, she came from behind, barreling right by, and brought the duck down on the field. I backed off gingerly. After half an hour, with a heavy crop, she flew to the cottonwood. Her work had been done for the day, dashing my hopes of seeing her hunt again, until tomorrow....

Margin of safety

If the queen sat on her cottonwood throne, it would quite soon become clear whether or not she was in a hunting mood. She seldom bothered to threaten ducks that were in the water, but as soon as they waddled up the shore or took flight, she leaned forward on the branch. Her chances of catching ducks depended very much on what they did next. Aware of their predicament on land, they quickly returned to water if they saw the falcon coming. There was, however, one fact of life that inexorably placed them at the mercy of their enemy; they had to eat. Dabbling species can find sustenance in marshes, but there is no food in the pools of rainwater that temporarily flood ploughed fields, except if they inundate standing crops. Swimming safely among cabbages and brussels sprouts, the ducks have a field day to the despair of the local farmer. Hundreds of mallards, pintails, wigeon and teal, happily eating day and night, quickly reduce the vegetables to bare stalks. Eventually, if all accessible plants have been ravaged, and even more so after the waters retreat, the fowl need to venture closer to land.

Wigeon are especially fond of tender grass that keeps growing all winter if the weather stays mild. Reluctant to fly overland when the sky has eyes, they spend the day on deep water and become active at night. They love the rain and when low meadows are sheeted by a steady downpour, the ducks gain a safe home base right on their feeding grounds. Nearest to the water the young shoots soon become cropped down to the ground. Greedily competing with each other, the hungry hordes move farther and farther up the meadow, like a herd of tiny cattle, babbling excitedly in their high-pitched voices.

The cottonwood queen has been watching the ducks with keen anticipation. If she flew too early, they would retreat in time. It was crucial to allow them a period of freedom so that they widened their distance from water and decreased their margin of safety. Attacks, even if they failed, would make them increasingly wary and on edge. This is why the queen could not share her hunting ground with other duck hunters. The less disturbance the better. At times, she might be quite careless herself, pressing her attack too soon and too often. Leaving the tree, she launched fast surprise attacks low over the ground. But before she had reached the target, the ducks rose and rushed to the safety of deeper water. Returning to her perch, she tried again a little later with the same lack of result. Her approach was now noticed well before she got anywhere close. It was as if the prey were thinking: "Oh, here comes the old bother again!" The more ducks there were, far and near, the earlier the flocks flushed, aborting her chances. Sometimes it seemed as if the falcon did not care. Perhaps she was just having fun. In contrast, if she was serious, she moved to another spot where she had not attacked for hours, and she became still, biding her time.

If I saw the cottonwood queen fly to one of the highest perches on the skyline, the bare snag of a giant spruce, I knew she was ready to kill. Knowing where the ducks were, I judged her chances and waited, binoculars glued to my eyes.

Stealth missile

On the crest of the wooded hill, the falcon snag was set well back from the fields and so high that the perched bird, as seen through the glasses, was just visible on the skyline. Unless you knew where to find her, you would never identify the tiny dot as a peregrine. I checked the snag often, especially if I had not seen the falcon for some time. One late afternoon, when the number of ducks in the area was low, I decided to keep an eye on an isolated flock of wigeon and mallards in a marshy corner of the fields. During the day, the ducks snoozed on deep water but toward evening they approached the shallows, attracted by grass sprouting in the muddy soil. Looking up at the snag, my heart skipped a beat; the falcon had arrived! From her skyline lookout, she had a great view of the marsh.

I had parked the car just off the narrow road that transected the fields. Instead of risking disturbance by going outside and setting up the scope, I stayed inside, my neck craned sideways at an uncomfortable angle, looking out of the open window. She took her time while I felt my back and shoulders stiffen. To relieve the tension, I shifted position and stole a quick glance at the ducks. Chattering and wheezing happily, the brightly colored innocents were outdoing each other, waddling farther up the shore where the grass was greener. Aiming the binoculars again at the falcon, I was just in time to see her spread her wings, but as soon as she dropped below the tree tops, she became invisible. Guessing the trajectory of her path, I kept the glasses steady until she showed up as a white dot against the dark background. The dot slowly dilated. Following the contour of the hillside, she fell like a cruise missile, wings swept back, approaching at great velocity. I did not dare move either my head or the glasses and peeked over the top of the binoculars just as she flashed by. Instantly, the whistled calls of wigeon swelled to an alarm. A wall of birds rushed into the air with the sound of a wind storm. She slammed into them, vanishing. I found her back standing in water up to her belly. Flapping her wings, she dragged her submerged victim toward the edge.

Through the glasses, in the brightest detail, I watched her kill the struggling drake. After his spasms died, she looked about for a minute, savage and wary, then she got to work hurriedly, plucking feathers and gulping down red meat. Seldom did I enjoy a more intimate view of the duck hawk on her kill, blood dripping from her hooked beak.

Occasionally, cars and farm trucks rumbled by on the road. One stopped. Perhaps the falcon had been spotted, or perhaps these people were just viewing the swans in the marsh? To my relief, the vehicle soon pulled away again and the falcon had not flinched. She continued to feed ravenously, pausing frequently to look about. Sated, she fussed over the carcass and dragged it a little farther up the muddy shore. She left suddenly, her wing beats scattering feathery down that floated back down onto the mud.

Sinking ankle-deep into the soft ground, I examined the wigeon drake, lying on his back. Only the fatty skin of the neck and part of the breast had been consumed. The meat looked clean and appetizing.

Perched on a branch of the lone cottonwood tree, the queen was picking her toes and cleaning her bill, rubbing it from side to side on the wood. Then she fluffed her feathers and relaxed as if nothing had happened, the low sun shining on her bulging throat, white and immaculate.

Weather and water

The number of ducks in the enclave varied greatly, depending on the weather and the amount of standing water. During dry spells, there were only half a dozen irrigation ponds that attracted waterfowl in small numbers. Mallards were usually the most common, coming and going openly, but the local peregrines showed no interest in them. They clearly preferred smaller species, including divers such as hooded merganser, bufflehead and ring-necked duck, but these were impossible to catch unless in flight. When the duck population was low, the cottonwood queen spent hours waiting for her opportunity. If she saw a distant chance, she dropped off her branch and accelerated hurriedly, wings sweeping at maximum power. Following her in the glasses, it was a thrill to sight her target. On two occasions I saw her intercept and seize a single wigeon flying low over the fields. But most often the ducks reached water in time.

To break the boredom of inactivity or to cope with chilly temperatures, I walked about and attempted to flush prey for her. She still mistrusted me if I got too close to her tree, but she watched with casual interest if I kept some distance. She probably considered me a harmless scavenger that could at times be useful. If I put up a duck, she took off in pursuit without hesitation. She obviously understood cause and effect; if I was at the far end of the fields, heading for a pond, she approached in anticipation, choosing a perch closer by. Nevertheless, more often than not, she failed to overtake the prey before it dropped into the next waterhole. And very soon also the ducks got wise to my treachery. As soon as they saw the falcon coming, they quickly returned to the pond. Or they refused to flush at all and simply rushed low over the water to the other side of the pond! After a while I stopped trying, not wanting to disappoint the falcon, quite apart from unfairly harassing the ducks. Too much disturbance might cause them to leave the area. It was better to let nature take its course.

The predator-prey equation changed if the wind turned easterly and brought Arctic air down from across the mountains. During the long night, the waters cooled quickly and began to freeze. If the cold persisted, the last of the fowl became sitting ducks, huddled together on the edge of a waterhole. The queen flushed them at will. Pursued in flight they vainly tried to find safety and dropped down on frozen ponds, where the falcon grabbed them point-blank. After snow covered the ground, masses of hungry ducks arrived from the north and descended on fields where crops were left standing. The falcon knew where to find them and executed her attack with cool precision. She was especially deadly if she could approach unseen from behind a hedge or a fence line where reedgrass grew tall. If the stealth attack terminated at a great distance from me, I would see hundreds of ducks rise in panic while she dropped out of sight. Finding her back on a kill was almost an anticlimax. One early morning, she used the raised roadbed as cover, skimming over the pavement just after I had walked by. She killed and fed on a duck by the edge of the ditch while cars passed by a few yards away at the rate of several each minute.

When the weather warmed again and meltwater collected in the depressions of fields and meadows, the ducks gathered by the hundreds, sometimes thousands. The more there were, the more trouble the peregrine seemed to have in making a catch since her approach was soon noticed. And the more difficulty I experienced in keeping her in view. It was frustrating to lose sight of her, screened behind masses of fleeing birds. When peace and quiet reigned again, she might be gone, perhaps having made a kill out of sight, or she might have returned to the cottonwood.

Hunting in the rain

On dark and rainy mornings, I dreaded the boredom of being confined to the vehicle, perhaps all day. Yet, giving in to my singular obsession, I headed for the field and reasoned that the falcon would make no exception either. What would she do? Peregrines certainly can stand a lot of rain. They might even enjoy it. On the prairies I watched them sit out torrential thunder showers. Perched on a fence post in the open, one bird flapped its wings as if using the opportunity for a welcome bath. After the storm had passed it roused its feathers and preened contentedly. On the West Coast, falcons do not hesitate to hunt during rain. As described by Frank Beebe, the Peale's peregrines of the Queen Charlotte Islands have a peculiar, bluish film of powder on their feathers that repels water like the back of a duck.

One very wet morning, after arrival in the enclave, I parked on the shoulder of the road and opened the window on the side away from the driving rain to scan the cottonwood and other known perches. She was not there. It seemed that she had more sense than I. Perhaps she was well fed and sitting out the storm on a sheltered cliff? Perhaps she had anticipated the change in weather and made a kill late last night?

The rain did not bother the ducks, on the contrary. Overnight some wigeon had arrived from the sea and settled down in the marsh by the road. Rising water levels would soon bring the grassy margin within safe reach. Nattering and whistling, they moved closer and closer. They were the lure that might attract the peregrine, sooner or later! In anticipation, I parked in a spot that gave a good view of the marsh as well as the cottonwood. When the falcon came by, I missed seeing her but the ducks suddenly retreated with a loud rush of wings and splashing water. Presently I found her on the tree. Now, having a focus for my observations, I did not mind the rain all that much. And during the course of the day, I was to see this falcon, usually so successful, in a very different light.

From time to time, she made an aborted attempt to capture ducks on the edge of the marsh. They always escaped into deep water. I sometimes missed her takeoff, but after a brief absence she was back on her perch. One flight was aimed at a few wigeon which had joined a group of trumpeter swans that were digging up and hammering carrots on a waterlogged field. As is their habit, the wigeon scavenged the crumbs. When the falcon made a low pass at them, they hid between their giant benefactors and refused to flush! The swans paid the peregrine no heed.

By late afternoon, while the rain continued, the falcon moved to a wooden powerpole along the road, a mere twenty yards (18 m) away from my car! She was now much closer to the marsh, but her chances looked equally dim. The ducks were all too aware of their peril. Once in a while, she made a threatening but futile pass and returned to the pole. The whistling calls of the wigeon sounded like derisive laughter. She sat with her back turned toward me. Through the glasses I noticed that her wings and tail were soaking wet. If she glanced to the side or backward, I briefly saw her face and she looked very unlike the bird I knew. Thin and bedraggled, she had lost all royal splendor, but her eyes were as bright and alert as ever. She had been on the lookout for prey since early morning and by now she must be very hungry indeed.

At dusk she suddenly flew to a pole in the middle of the fields, some distance away. From there she would be able to see a marshy corner at the opposite end of the enclave, by the inlet of the drainage ditch which was the only other spot where I knew there were some ducks. Setting up the telescope in the car, I focused and could just make her out, hunched up on the side arm of the wooden pole. She stayed there until the last light dimmed. When she finally dropped off her perch, her shimmering shape vanished at once going in the direction of the marsh. In my mind's eye, I saw her streak across the water, coming out of the dark, driving the ducks toward land, cutting off their escape.

I did not follow her; it was too dark, too far and too wet. Next morning just after first light, I went to search for her kill. A red-tailed hawk had already found it. Carrying the carcass, he rose heavily from the edge of the marsh. A bed of wigeon feathers lay on the mud, plastered down by last night's rain.

The beauty and the terror

Each winter, the enclave was hunted over by at least five different peregrines. In the absence of the cottonwood queen, one or more interlopers might come down for a quick kill any time of the day. One of the larger falcons did not look like a *F. p. pealei*. Her chest was not white with teardrop spots, but salmon-colored like a typical *F. p. anatum*. Her feet were bright orange-yellow. The first time I saw her sitting on wet ploughland, one sunny morning, I was stunned by her beauty! She was also a spectacular hunter. On a blustery day when a rain squall made me hurry back to the road and I involuntarily flushed hundreds and hundreds of ducks from the marsh, she added greatly to the tumult, zigzagging back and forth after a careening bunch of teal. Capturing one of them in a violent display of wing power, she landed on the edge of a field nearby. Just then the high wind shredded the clouds and a low sun broke through with prairie brightness. Standing on her prey, she looked resplendent, her chest aglow in orange-gold.

This *anatum* beauty also succeeded with flying colors in a classic hunt from soar, one of very few I have seen in this area. After watching her for well over an hour, a tiny white speck on a distant tree, she finally went into action and climbed to a soaring pitch high over the fields. Suddenly, she furled her wings and descended in a flat, mile-long stoop to overtake a pair of ring-necked ducks and seize the drake from behind, as if he had not been moving at all. Luckily for her, no eagle had seen what I had seen and she ate her fill undisturbed.

Even more impressive as duck hunters were the medium-sized peregrines that occasionally visited the enclave. Although I never knew for certain whether these were small tundra females or large Peale's males, I think they were the latter since they reminded me strongly of the tiercels I had seen on Langara Island. One of these slender interlopers was just terrific! Instead of taking a sitting duck by surprise or approaching a flying target in its blind spot, from behind and below, he met the flocks openly, high in the sky.

Outflying his prey in grand style, he drove them right down to the ground. A fantastic series of high altitude hunts, that made my mouth dry with excitement and admiration, was launched from the cottonwood. Taking off at a blistering pace, his long wings flicking steadily, the tiercel headed directly for a string of ducks approaching over the distant skyline. When I finally spotted them in the glasses, they were still no more than tiny specks. Describing a wide half-circle, climbing all the while, the peregrine turned to follow the flock that continued on its way toward the fields. As he began to draw level, the ducks veered aside and separated, descending. The tiercel zeroed in on a teal, following it down. Just as he closed in, his target changed course abruptly and the chase went out of sight behind bushes. The teal must have reached water just in time because the tiercel came back empty-footed.

The next two hunts were also launched at ducks approaching high over the skyline. A female pintail, hotly pursued on her way to the fields, managed to find cover behind trees, out of sight. But a drake was not so lucky. Closely followed by the tiercel, he went down into a wet depression, both dropping out of view in the rank grass. Presently, while I kept the glasses trained on the spot, the peregrine emerged again and an adult bald eagle came down from the sky to retrieve the drake!

While all three of the above hunts had been started from the cottonwood, the tiercel was now perched on a wooden power pole along the road, right in front of my car. He flew off again soon, but not to start another long-range attack. Instead, he pursued an immature tiercel carrying a prey! This peregrine was noticeably smaller than the terrific tiercel and he quickly dropped the food item in midair. The adult caught it at once and carried it back to the pole. However, to my surprise, he only nudged it briefly and resumed spying for ducks.

Fixing his gaze on the skyline, he fluttered his wings in anticipation. He had spotted prey but restrained himself, waiting for the right moment to launch forth. Seconds later, the same scenario unfolded as before. Meeting the ducks very high over the hills, the tiercel follow-chased a teal back down over the fields. There, he was joined by the immature tiercel! Alternately, they swooped in a frenzy of furious wingbeats until the adult caught the teal low over the ground. Descending at once, he was out of sight behind some stubble. Presently, when I approached too closely, he carried his prey to a tree. On the spot from where he had flushed, I found a few iridescent green feathers and the head of the teal, the eyes still wide open in terror....

On my way back to the car, I looked at the flat-topped power pole by the road. The small prey was still there. But a little later it ended up at the base of the pole, blown off by a gust of wind. It was a robin, a beautiful specimen, its breast deep red, not a feather out of place.

A test of patience

In the last winter of observation in the enclave, after the drainage schemes had done their damage, there remained only one large sheet of water that was at its widest point about 300 yards (250 m) across. In the marshy corner where the ditch entered, there were a couple of hundred ducks including a few dozen green-winged teal. On the first day after my arrival in the area, I saw a bald eagle fly over the marsh and as a result all of the waterfowl took wing. Suddenly, a peregrine, fast and straight as an arrow, seized a teal and turned away at once. As I followed it in the glasses, it disappeared far away over the wooded crest of the valley, the eagle in hot pursuit.

This was a delightful and encouraging start of my study period, as well as rare evidence that the actions of the ponderous eagle, albeit involuntarily, sometimes benefit the speedy falcon! If only these two winged hunters, with their complementary abilities, would cooperate instead of compete; the eagle as the beater, flushing ducks from the water, and the falcon overtaking them in flight!

This last winter, which began with such promise, turned into a frustrating but revealing experience that sorely tested my patience. As before, there was one dominant falcon in the enclave and she concentrated her attention on the inlet marsh. Each morning at first light, just after I parked on the muddy track bordering the fields, I found her in a large tree, not on one of the top branches but somewhere in the middle of the dense crown. Keeping the glasses focused on her hulking shape, I waited hour after hour and saw her make several low attacks over the water. She never caught anything while I watched, but several times I missed her takeoff and found her back on her perch plucking prey. The ground below the tree was littered with the wings of green-winged teal.

After heavy rain, hundreds of ducks congregated in a flooded section of an adjacent field and I could not resist shooing them into the air. The falcon left her perch at once while the sky filled with mallards, pintails and wigeon, but no teal. Without making the slightest attempt at chasing any of the bigger ducks, she turned back, obviously only interested in a prey that she could carry to her tree, out of reach of eagles. Unlike mine, her patience seemed unlimited. As the day wore on, her robust profile became slimmer, feathers sleek against her body, and I began to wonder whether this bird was perhaps a tiercel after all? But my doubts were dispelled later, after she had eaten and returned to her normal shape. Periodically she abruptly gave up her vigil and flew away over the crest of the hills. In the valley beyond was another marsh with some ducks, including teal. Later in the day, I might suddenly find her back on her perch, sometimes with prey in her talons. I never found out how she managed to catch them. Since the local teal were loath to leave the water, she might have struck them on the surface. This is the way the Peale's peregrines of the Queen Charlotte Islands hunt murrelets and other small ocean divers as described in the previous chapter.

When it was time to terminate the last winter of observation in the enclave, I was not all that sorry to leave. For, quite apart from the drainage schemes that had ruined most of the wetland, there had been too many other annoyances. The parcel of land adjacent to the inlet marsh was a meeting place for the city's model airplane club. On most days, radio-controlled toys circled over the water and fields, producing a high-pitched whine that became increasingly irritating. Neither the ducks nor the peregrine seemed to pay any attention to the careening models or their earsplitting noise. She even ignored the people and cars that passed by below her tree, which stood right by the entrance of the field. In turn, the hobbyists were oblivious to the falcon and the high drama unfolding around them.

Yet, when my observations drew to a close, I felt a twinge of sadness to leave this place where I had enjoyed so many fascinating adventures. If there was one consolation at all, it was that peregrines apparently have more patience and tolerance for human disturbance than I. No doubt, their kind would continue to hunt over this intensely managed corner of paradise as long as people left them alone and as long as there were ducks or other birds to prey upon.

The prey's paradox

While the big Peale's falcons, males as well as females, hunted ducks by preference, there were other tiercels wintering in the enclave that were noticeably smaller. They took mainly passerines, such as robins and blackbirds. One adult male, tiny enough to be a tundra peregrine, was very accomplished. He seemed to have much time to spare and sat for hours on a high snag, mobbed by chickadees and finches. To make a kill, all he needed was one fair chance. Taking off at speed, he met a lone robin head-on and plucked it out of the air without further ado. Another robin, also met head-on, plunged down in the critical moment, but the tiercel stooped after it and caught it before it had dropped halfway to the ground.

The immature males were more fun to watch. Far from shy, they allowed me to approach closely. Sometimes I stood right below their tree. Through the glasses, in intimate detail, they looked harmless and docile, preening and stretching their wings. But as soon as they sprang off their perch, they were all spunk and speed, giving their utmost. Time and again, they attacked flocks of blackbirds and starlings, but their sentinels cried alarm in time. Flushing, the flocks bunched tightly together for protection and took cover in trees around the farms where they felt safe and scolded the impudent but scary predator. The young tiercels never seemed to succeed, unless they bided their time and used the right strategy.

Taking off from a tree, in an indirect approach, one immature male attacked a lone robin on the far side of a wide field. He first angled away at about forty-five degrees along a hedge, then turned sharply with the sun at his back. Descending gradually at terrific speed, he flushed the robin from the grass and gathered it in his feet as if there was nothing to it. By contrast, another immature male went about it the hard way. Taking off from a tree, he launched a prolonged pursuit of a snipe passing by high in the sky. The hunt carried far out of sight and included numerous close passes. In this contest between falcon and prey, neither strategy nor luck played favorites. The swiftest would survive another day.

It was remarkable that the local peregrines never bothered with several other prey species common in the area. Apart from the glaucous-winged gulls, which were too bulky to mess with for any falcon, there were dainty mew gulls that collected in flooded meadows after heavy rain. They were seldom harassed and I never saw them taken, nor did I find any feather remains. Neither was there any evidence that the falcons hunted crows. Each evening, thousands came by in a straggling stream on the way to their roost, but they too seemed immune from attack. Even pigeons, the classical peregrine staple in many other regions, were apparently of little interest to these falcons. The cottonwood queen never looked twice at them, but in her absence some interlopers did. One adult female, approaching in the cover of trees and buildings, grabbed a courting dove out of the air before it knew what happened. An adult tiercel pursued and caught a feral pigeon over the fields. When I examined the half-eaten carcass later, I noticed that a hand-full of grain had spilled from the pigeon's torn crop, a heavy load, which might have turned the scales in the falcon's favor. A local pigeon fancier told me that his flocks were often attacked in early fall, especially by young falcons, and he had learned the hard way to release his precious birds before they had eaten! It seems a paradox that a good meal can lead to fatal consequences, be they pigeons gorging on grain or ducks leaving the safety of water for the delights of sprouting grass.

Chapter 10

Might Is Right

Although ignored or tolerated by humans, the falcons wintering in the agricultural enclave on Vancouver Island did not lack for enemies. Among these were two pairs of red-tailed hawks. Unobtrusive, they usually hid in the foliage of spruce woods and they hunted in their own sneaky way, occasionally even grabbing a duck. One day a red-tail dropped out of a tree and pinned down a wigeon on the grass below. Surprisingly, after a minute or so the hawk released its victim and returned to its perch! Perhaps it was not hungry enough to bother with plucking? In their relationship with the local peregrines, the red-tails were quite unpredictable, perhaps also depending on the state of their appetite. Sometimes they left the falcon alone, at other times they drew near soon after she had made a kill.

The cottonwood queen hated the hawks. Cacking menacingly, she flew out to meet them, but they were quick to take cover in a tree. The branches shielded them from her stoops. After she went back to her kill, the hawks waited calmly until she was finished and left. However, they treated the smaller peregrines with far less respect. One winter day, when snow covered the fields, the pair did not hesitate to rob an adult tiercel that had just killed a pintail drake. In turn, the red-tails were soon interrupted by a rough-legged hawk. After all three of them had their fill, the waiting tiercel flew down from his tree perch to get his share. There could not have been much left!

The most numerous freeloaders were glaucous-winged gulls. Like the hawks, their interest in the falcon's kill varied. On some days they paid no attention. And if they did, there was seldom more than one bird at the time. A little larger than the peregrine and armed with a huge yellow bill, the gull was a formidable but discrete presence. It waited its turn, albeit with increasing impatience, sidling closer step by step. The falcon ignored her bold visitor. After she departed, the gull quickly hacked the carcass to pieces, leaving nothing but wings and bones.

While the cottonwood queen had enough clout to keep hungry gulls and buteos at bay, she could do little about other contenders. One day, her fresh kill was appropriated by a male gyrfalcon, not much bigger than the peregrine. She cackled and made a few angry passes, then retreated to a pole by the road. Having finished eating, the gyr probably left enough of the pintail duck for the queen's rightful share. The cookie crumbled along very different lines with eagles, the biggest and greediest thieves of all!

The eagle's ransom

Perched high on a hillside tree, overlooking the ocean beyond as well as inland fields, there was not much that escaped the eagle's eye. When the regal bird turned its white head and directed its steady gaze downward, the spiky feathers on its nape bristled in the breeze. Far below, the cottonwood queen had just seized a wigeon on the edge of floodwater. The eagle waited a few minutes, long enough to give the peregrine time to kill her prey.

When the falcon saw her familiar foe coming, she uttered a plaintive protest and abandoned her quarry at once. She did not even bother confronting the great bird. Without stopping, the eagle reached out a yellow foot and lifted the dead duck off the grass, carrying it back to its lofty lookout. A second eagle that had followed at a distance now fell in line with its mate, hoping to share the spoils of this brazen act of piracy.

Naturally, as it had been on Langara and elsewhere, might was right. Here on the winter fields, the peregrine, willy-nilly, played the role of great provider to a host of lesser predators and scavengers. But the eagle, a calculating profiteer, demanded his ransom from the top. The unequal balance of power between the two had developed over millions of years of parallel evolution, and the peregrine was not to be discouraged, even though it had to hunt and kill far more than its own needs. Here on the island, bald eagles were common and inescapable. Unless their attention was turned elsewhere, they seldom allowed the falcon a chance to eat much from her kill, if at all.

Once I watched the cottonwood queen from dawn to dusk and saw her capture three wigeon, the first one around nine o'clock, the second one an hour or so later. She lost both. Each time the falcon returned to the cottonwood. Finally, just before dusk, she managed to catch her third wigeon. This time no eagles showed up. Perhaps they had left already for a distant roost.

On occasion, even the golden eagle, rare on the coast, tried to get away with robbery, if bigger bullies let him! Just after the cottonwood queen had nailed a wigeon in a muddy field of corn stubble, an adult male golden eagle materialized out of the blue, landing on the duck. He took off at once, pursued by an adult bald. Unable to rise quickly enough, the golden was forced to relinquish his ill-gotten booty. Incidentally, this splendid male was perfectly capable of catching his own ducks. A few days earlier, I had seen him wing majestically across the corn field and take a drake out of a flock of mallards rising in front of him. The eagle ate his fill, sunlight gleaming on his golden hackles and on the green head of his prey. Soon after, his leftovers were collected by a bald eagle, patrolling the fields and keeping tabs on other scavengers.

A society of thieves

After I had left Vancouver Island I found bald eagles even more common at Boundary Bay on the mainland coast. At low tide, dozens could be seen sitting on the mudflats. One morning, I counted 128 from one observation point! Of course, watching these splendid birds, especially if no falcons were within view, was a pleasure and a privilege in its own right. The eagles' daily routine was dictated by the tides. At high water, the ponderous predators saved energy and perched on trees. At ebb time, they spread out over the intertidal zone, searching the exposed ocean floor for fish and other food items. Here, as on Langara, they spied on the activities of the glaucous-winged gulls. As soon as one of these hovered and descended, one or more eagles hurried over for a look. Pursuing and robbing the gull, they were always ready to seize and kill the bird itself should it show signs of weakness. The eagles also hunted waterfowl, swooping down repeatedly at any duck or diver slow to get out of the way.

Immature eagles seemed superior at retrieving prey from the water; their relatively large wings allowed them to hover with greater ease than the compact adults. However, the latter were faster, more agile and more dominant. Any lucky hunter was immediately accosted by others. Often a duck changed "hands" several times. The first to eat were surrounded by envious onlookers. Uncertain, some eagles carried their duck aloft and took a few bites in midflight, swallowing large chunks before they were forced to drop the remains at the command of a more aggressive contender.

Also here, this aquiline society of buccaneers exerted a strong influence over the wintering peregrines. Always hungry and hopeful, rarely succeeding, they even pursued falcons with prey as small as sandpipers. If a peregrine had driven a dunlin into cover, eagles approached hurriedly to locate the cowering bird in tall grass or other vegetation where it was safe from the falcon but not from the eagle.

However, the unforgiving code that might is right was not the prerogative of the white-headed scoundrels. One day, to my great surprise, a female prairie falcon got the better of a peregrine! This dry-country species is a very unusual sight on the northern coast. Perched on a piece of driftwood in the distance, it had at first been mistaken for an immature peregrine. While I kept an eye on it, an adult tiercel stooped at a flushing flock of dunlins nearby and caught a single bird that separated from the others. As I followed the peregrine in the binoculars, an astonishing sideshow developed. The other falcon turned up in hot pursuit, giving me a clear view of its diagnostic, black underwing linings. A notch bigger than the tiercel, the prairie was obviously a female. She was also faster. The peregrine soon released his prey, which dropped a few feet, then spread its wings and flew on with the prairie hot on its tail! As a last resort, the dunlin plunged into a tussock of saltgrass, to be retrieved in a flash by the pirate and carried back to her driftwood perch.

Some fifteen minutes later, after she had plucked and consumed her stolen meal, the prairie falcon took off again over the mudflats, climbing steadily, in pursuit of an adult male peregrine, probably the same one as before. He was carrying a small prey. High over the ocean, the prairie finally gave up and returned to shore. Considering that she had just eaten and that her kind was definitely capable of catching its own sandpipers, this falcon was obviously no better than the greediest of eagles!

Chapter 11

Tide Water Spectacle

After my observations in the farmland enclave on Vancouver Island had become less enjoyable and productive because of increased human disturbance and the negative impacts of the drainage ditch, I searched for a more natural study area along the coast. The rugged outlines of Vancouver Island include several estuaries, rich in bird life and accessible by road, but their shores are broken up by industrial and housing developments, with the result that public access is restricted. My search eventually led to the lower mainland of the province.

Within sight of the highrises of metropolitan Vancouver lies Boundary Bay, a ten-mile (16 km) expanse of shallows, bounded at either end by forested headlands and protected by an offshore archipelago of mountainous islands. At low tide, the water retreats almost out of sight. The mudflats, washed over and replenished by the ocean twice daily, are the feeding grounds for hundreds of thousands of migratory shorebirds that stop over in seasonal waves. During winter, the number of species is comparatively low. The plaintive calls of a few black-bellied plover pierce the frequent mist, and the odd killdeer or snipe graces the edge of the saltmarsh, but the only common species of sandpiper is the dunlin. In winter, its plumage is nondescript, counter-shaded for camouflage, gray above and white below.

A citizen of the world, the dunlin breeds on circumpolar tundras and migrates far down the Atlantic and Pacific coasts. A portion of its huge population goes no farther south than the rain-shrouded lower coast of British Columbia. Here in the bay, from October to March, their hordes often exceed 30,000. They are the major prey of peregrines, which is quite surprising because the dunlin is hardly

140

bigger than a sparrow and weighs less than two ounces (45 g). To meet its caloric demand, the peregrine has to catch several of these tiny sandpipers each day, no mean task, since the dunlin is an extremely erratic flyer. Its antipredator strategies have been honed over the millennia with selective precision. In this wide-open coastal habitat, a dynamic ecosystem created by the interplay of water and land, I saw the peregrine employ its most awesome speed and power.

Instead of watching perched falcons and waiting for them to start hunting, which had been my main method of observation on Vancouver Island, my usual strategy on the coast was simply to keep an eye on the prey. If flocks of dunlins took to the sky, drawing together in fear, I tried to spot the cause of the alarm, a peregrine or its smaller but no less deadly cousin, the merlin. With luck I might see them hunt, far away or very close by. During rainy or windy weather, I did a lot of watching from the parked car. On fair days, I walked for hours on the low dike that separates the bay from the low-lying inland fields. Apart from the weather, my routines were ruled by the tides, as they were for the birds. At low water, the dunlins withdrew almost out of sight. However, a few hours later, the upcoming tide would inexorably force them back to the dike. Their fortunes came and went with the ever-shifting water line. Superimposed on this relentless force, which alternately opened up and locked away their food supply, was the inescapable need to cope with predation.

Thirty thousand sandpipers

Over the shore far to the west, thousands of dunlins are up in the air. Their dense, globular flocks roll back and forth across the skyline like giant wheels. Tightly packed together, the birds turn all at once, alternately flashing silver and black like a semaphore sending warning signals that make distant birds rise in uneasy response. For a brief moment, I see a larger speck among them, soon lost in the milling crowd. Was it a falcon? Gradually, the birds separate and descend low over the water, until all signs of unrest have gone.

If the uproar had indeed been caused by a hunting falcon, it might have made a kill and landed somewhere to eat. On the other hand, if its attack had failed, the raptor might follow the shore and come my way. Sitting down on a driftwood log on the edge of the saltmarsh, I alternately scan the sky to the west and keep an eye on the mudflats nearby where thousands of dunlins are feeding, hungrily following the ebbing water line. The busy little birds seem blissfully ignorant of their peril. Many minutes pass in utter calm. The suspense dissolves and I relax into idle reverie.

A long line of dunlins begins to lift off the mud, swelling like a sail into the wind. Are they just moving up with the receding tide, or have they spotted the enemy? A sweeping view to the west reveals nothing. Looking back at the dunlins, I see that the flock has coalesced into a dense vertical column, shaking and twisting like an angry serpent. High over them, black and menacing against the gray sky, a tiercel wings back and forth. Looking for an opening, he makes a feint, denting the flock, and shoots back up to his high pitch. Suddenly, he cartwheels with rigid wings and stoops straight down, his aim near the bottom edge of the dense mass of dunlins. Almost colliding, he reverses direction at once. At his next stoop, the column begins to sag and caves in, flattening out over the waves. Strafed again and again, several dunlins drop out, splashing into the water. They get up and away again in the next instant, dodging the swooping peregrine. Regaining altitude with frenzied wing beats, the tiercel turns back for another pass at an isolated bird, overtaking his fleeing target in a split second. He again fails to connect. But he is not giving up yet....

While the lone dunlin is zigzagging low over the mud, on the way to the shore, a gull and a harrier take up the chase. To my astonishment, they are joined by an adult bald eagle, all of them in hot pursuit of the tiny prey. Undeterred, bypassing his contenders, the tiercel keeps on stooping. He hits! The dunlin bounces onto the mud and lies still. But it is not the peregrine that reaps his just reward. In an instant, the small bundle is picked up and carried along by the eagle, without stopping.

The tiercel leaves at once and by the time I find him again in the glasses, he is dwindling in size, hurrying east. Far away, he descends obliquely low over the flats while the sky above fills with flocking dunlins. Lowering the glasses, I notice that the shore nearby, where thousands of sandpipers had been feeding a few minutes ago, is all but deserted. Presently, a peregrine comes back into view from the east, high, at terrific speed. Hurtling down past me, beating his wings in furious bursts close to the tail, he streaks low over the mudflats for hundreds of yards and slashes through a flushing stream of dunlins. Failing to strike, he ascends again into the gray sky and begins a similar attack far away, vanishing from sight.

The champion slugger

Awed by the violence I have just witnessed, I replay the events before my mind's eye, attempting to recall the correct sequence and exact detail, so that I can describe them in my bulging notebook. Both flights probably involved the same tiercel. There were a series of hunts, but I could be sure of the outcome in only two. Interpreting the facts conservatively, the stoop at the flock and subsequent pursuit of the single dunlin qualified as one hunt, a successful one, although the kill had been pirated by the eagle. The long-distance pass at the feeding flock of dunlins, a few minutes later, constituted another hunt, an unsuccessful surprise attack. Thus far, as of 1998, over four winters, I have tallied a total of 302 hunts, of which twenty-eight ended up in captures, but no two were exactly alike.

Over the years, it became plain there was much variation in hunting style between individual peregrines. The star of the dramatic sequence described above was certainly an accomplished individual. He had not minded approaching openly, attacking flocks

143

that had become aware of his approach. Over the course of two weeks, I saw him hunting nearly every day, always in the same classic and hardhitting style. Each time, the chase was joined by gulls, harriers and eagles. They apparently knew what to expect and were keen on taking advantage of prey that was struck down.

One day, while I sat quietly on a driftwood log in the morning sun, the adult tiercel, hunting over the mudflats, scattered a flock of dunlins and singled out one of them for a prolonged pursuit. Seeking cover, the prey approached the shore, but at the sixth or seventh stoop, the confused little bird alighted on the mud, short of the marsh grass. At his next pass, the peregrine kicked the cowering dunlin like a football, flinging it back up into the air before it fell back like a wet rag. Next moment, the lifeless carcass was snatched up by an adult eagle which had been following closely behind! All this happened right in front of my seat!

Clearly, this tiercel was determined to smack his prey, a killing style I had seldom witnessed anywhere. On the coast, most adult males simply seized the dunlin in their feet. And they used far less spectacular hunting styles than the champion slugger. Their way was to approach very low and capitalize on surprise, exerting a minimum of effort. Prey was taken directly from behind as it lifted off the ground, unless it managed to veer aside in the nick of time.

Easy does it

One winter, the resident adult male showed a very different preference. He appeared to ignore the huge gatherings of sandpipers on the tide line. Perhaps he found them too much trouble. If attacked, they would spot him soon and flush well ahead, massing together in defensive formations. Instead, flying along the edge of the saltmarsh, this tiercel was keen on isolated groups or individuals. With practiced ease, he snatched his victim from the tail end of flocks that flushed just ahead. He also proved very agile in chasing single birds, overtaking them quickly if they tried to escape high into the sky. Forcing them down, he seized them in one or two lightning passes low over the water. Hunting by stealth, he kept a low profile, drawing little attention to himself from potential pirates. This was obviously an old pro, yet even he lost some prey to the bald eagle.

On a rainy afternoon, while I sat in the car and scanned the shore through the glasses, I happened to pick up the tiercel chasing a single dunlin over a point of land. As he passed over a foursome of resting eagles, all of them sprang into the air to join the hunt. Seconds later, the desperate dunlin, dodging the falcon's pass, dropped into the saltgrass. Doubling back, inches ahead of the eagles, the tiercel attempted to snatch up his prey without alighting, but all he got for his efforts was a fistful of vegetation.

Another adult tiercel, or perhaps the same one, had acquired an even more unobtrusive and specialized habit; he hunted dunlins at night while they flew over a complex of brightly lit greenhouses. This unique discovery had been passed on to me by a local bird-watcher, Richard Swanston, who had observed several of these incidents over two winters. One evening, I accompanied him to the greenhouse, arriving just after dark. Like a bright star, the tiercel was cruising back and forth high over the buildings. In the course of about ten minutes, he made three fast passes at dunlins that flew by, illuminated from below. He failed to catch the skittish prey and eventually vanished into the dark. On an earlier date, Richard had seen him seize a sandpiper and pluck it on the wing, plumes floating down like fireflies. His meal finished, the tiercel had resumed hunting and caught a second prey, this time a small passerine.

Machine-gun tiercel

Each winter, the bay was hunted over by two or more immature peregrines. The tiercels displayed the full spectrum of tactics, as well as astounding stamina. No holding back here and no calculated attempts to stay out of sight! Flying high, they made one long-range surprise attack after the other, descending obliquely low over the flats, wings flicking in bursts close to the tail. Streaking through flushing flocks of dunlins, they tried to seize or hit them anyway they could. If a bird dropped out, dead or crippled, the tiercel turned around calmly to retrieve his prey from the water or mud. After the surprise advantage was lost, he might make a pass or two at a flee-ing dunlin, which usually saved itself adroitly. However, if truly aroused, the tiercel kept up the pursuit. Some dunlins managed to outmaneuver their enemy and escaped high into the sky. Others found safety in saltgrass on the shore.

Like the adults, the immature males included individuals with a characteristic and uncommon style. One very dark tiercel was even bolder than the champion slugger. I called him the machine-gun tiercel. After several threatening feints and a series of impetuous stoops, he forced the flocks low over the water. He then plummeted down just behind them, drew level and barreled right through the densely packed birds! Each time, a dozen or more dodged by dropping out in a pit-a-pat of splashes. It looked as if the flock had been raked by a burst of gunfire! The dunlins rose and got away again just as quickly, but some had obviously been hit. Turning back, the peregrine adroitly fished his victim out of the water. Carrying his prize, the successful tiercel would then either fly inland or disappear out of sight across the bay, retreating to a point where he could pluck his prey without interference from klepto-parasites and freeloaders.

The hunting method of the machine-gun tiercel looked very productive but might also be risky. What if he should collide with a dunlin the wrong way? The result could be wing damage or worse. In comparing the methods of the immature and the adult tiercel, it seemed to me that the equally fearless slugger had shown more restraint, prudently biding his time until single birds had separated from the flock.

Brute force

Despite their small size, dunlins were apparently quite satisfactory as the main prey for the local tiercels. But what about the females? Broad-shouldered and compact, some of the peregrines wintering here looked like the biggest Peale's falcons I had seen on Langara. (In fact, individuals recovered near Boundary Bay had been banded on the island.) Would these very large females bother to capture dunlins? One winter, an adult female made some impressive attempts. Perhaps she wanted a light afternoon snack. Leaving a driftwood perch, where she had idled away the midday hours, she climbed high into the sky with the steady and hurried beat typical of a peregrine that means business and that is so exciting to watch! Far away, over the low tide line, she fell steeply in a grand stoop.

Thousands of dunlins flushed in panic. Reversing her momentum, she threw up perpendicularly, towering high over the fleeing birds and stooping down just as steeply. Unsuccessful, she climbed back up and left, her long wings flicking at a steady pace. Setting her sights a mile away, she again fell from the sky like a thunderbolt.

On subsequent afternoons, this female flew on a straight course very high over the flats and stooped at sandpipers or plovers fleeing low above the water. All of them splashed down and she failed to catch any. I never saw her persist in pursuit. Her style reminded me of the maritime falcons I had watched flying high over the ocean at Langara. Perhaps she was more accustomed to hunting ducks and divers. But how would she ever get the chance of holding onto a duck here on this eagle-dominated coast? One afternoon, to my great surprise, she could not resist flushing half a dozen pintails from the edge of the saltmarsh. Chasing one of them out over the mud-flats, she caught it easily, seizing it directly from behind. Of course, the eagles had seen what I had seen! She surrendered the duck without protest and resumed her vigil on a piece of driftwood.

After sundown, hundreds of wigeon began to lift off the ocean, heading inland where they would wreak their nightly havoc on the farmer's meadow. I was watching the falcon through the telescope. When she finally took wing, it was so dark that I lost her shimmering shape at once.

Late-night hunting, after the eagles had gone to their roost, was no doubt the best strategy for duck-hunting peregrines here, particularly if they foraged inland in areas where their enemies were less common. However, on the coast, the smallest species of waterfowl that could be carried out of reach of the big pirates, remained tempting targets at anytime. Some falcons got lucky and picked off a bufflehead flying from one ditch to the other. Others hunted teal, which were quite scarce here in the shallows of the intertidal zone, perhaps because of the many falcons. A demonstration of how highly teal were desired came one afternoon when an immature tiercel began a vigorous climb to meet a large flock of mallards and pintails on their way to the ocean, approaching high over the inland. As he finally drew level, the peregrine turned to follow-chase the ducks. After he began passing dozens of mallards and pintails, it suddenly became clear that his aim was a single teal leading the flock! Descending gradually, he was inches from overtaking the little one when it plunged headlong into the water, saving itself from a fate that had seemed certain.

The dapper merlin

Less common or less visible in the bay than peregrines, the merlin often hunted unobtrusively low over the saltmarsh and inland fields, trying to take its prey by surprise. During high tide, the little falcon was easily missed or lost to view. Sneaky and quick, it sometimes had a dunlin in its talons before I saw it coming. Or it flushed a huge flock from the edge of the saltgrass and disappeared from sight among them. But at low tide, it also hunted far out over the mud-flats. Even here, it always tried a stealth approach first. It invariably failed, although it was astonishing to see how close it got before the alarm was sounded. While the dunlins bunched up into the sky, the tiny falcon pressed on and climbed high over the flock. Maneuvering for position, it executed feints and stoops in the same classic style as the best of peregrines. If a single dunlin separated from the flock, the merlin proved persistent in pursuit and more pre-cise than its larger cousin. The chase could carry on high, giving the quarry a fair chance to get away. However, if it ended low over the water, the dunlin was doomed. Dodging ten or twenty close passes, it frequently splashed down, taking off again in a different direction, until its luck ran out and the merlin stopped short, hovering over its exhausted victim.

Although I saw only twenty-nine hunts by merlins, seven of these ended in capture, a success rate of 17.2 percent. By compari-son, Page and Whitacre recorded 12.8 percent in 343 merlin hunts on the coast of California. There is another, more significant differ-ence between their data and mine. Page and Whitacre never saw captures made in extended aerial pursuits; all of their forty-four sandpiper kills were the product of surprise attacks. However, they watched only a single merlin, an adult female, which seized her prey the quick and easy way, perhaps unwilling to exert herself too much in long chases. By contrast, my observations involved a number of different merlins. As was already pointed out by Gustav Rudebeck, a study of predation should ideally involve many individuals of that species instead of only one or two which might lead to a biased or skewed conclusion. For further comparison, merlins at Beaverhills Lake achieved 12.6 percent success in 223 shorebird hunts, and here too, seven of the twenty-eight kills came after long pursuits.

Since prolonged and vigorous chases require the expense of much energy, it is important that perseverance be rewarded. This was never a sure thing for the merlins at Boundary Bay. To enjoy the benefit of their hard work, they still had to get back to shore and find a safe place to eat. They needed luck to escape from the envious eyes of others, such as the larger falcons. One peregrine already interfered with a merlin by taking over the last stage of a long chase. Gulls and harriers were also keen on joining hunts in progress. Others hurriedly approached the moment a capture had been achieved, although they gave up quickly once the merlin had reached maximum speed. Eagles were more persistent and hard to shake. Hotly pursued, several merlins, carrying their precious cargo, got away by flying between the banks of the ditch paralleling the dike. Another merlin, which had caught its dunlin far out over the flats, was set upon high in the sky for at least a mile. It refused to give up its prey even though the eagle was right on its tail and made pass after pass. Side-slipping each time, the agile merlin eventually reached a farm yard and disappeared between the buildings. In this uneven contest between David and Goliath, the dapper little falcon had clearly prevailed over the giant eagle!

Chapter 12

In Awe and Admiration

How do the hunting methods of the peregrines and merlins wintering on the coast compare to those of the migrants at Beaverhills Lake? On the surface, there seemed to be a great deal of difference. However, given the right set of habitat conditions, there were also striking similarities. As described in the preceding chapter, the tidewater falcons often attacked flocking dunlins in spectacular style, high in the sky. In fact, the vast majority of peregrine and merlin kills were made after such open attacks. By contrast, 80 percent of all kills by the Alberta falcons were the result of a stealth approach! This very significant difference is in my view a consequence of habitat and prey numbers. On the vast coastal mudflats, with birds everywhere, surprise at close range was difficult to achieve. So the falcons were forced to use an open approach. By comparison, at Beaverhills Lake mudflat habitat was usually quite limited in extent and the reedy margins made it very easy for hunting falcons to stay out of sight until the last moment. They were especially deadly on lone individuals and isolated small flocks. However, conditions changed during dry years when falling water levels led to a widening of mudflats. Then, the number of staging

shorebirds was greatest and hence surprise became all the more difficult to achieve. Under these circumstances the falcons were compelled to hunt openly, in the same spectacular manner as their kin on the coast, and they did not shy away from persistent pursuit! A good example of open-style attack is the falcon and phalarope show that took place far out over the lake, as described in chapter five. Conversely, coastal peregrines did not hesitate to capitalize on the element of surprise if the opportunity presented itself. This occurred during rising tides, when the dunlins were restricted to a narrowing strip of mud along the saltmarsh. Then, the falcons approached by stealth, low over the vegetation. Deadly efficient, they might seize a flushing dunlin at the first pass. The success rate of peregrines hunting over the saltmarsh was 33 percent, significantly higher than their rate of 8 percent in hunts over the open flats.

High-tide retreat

Given the fact that the saltmarsh was just too dangerous a place to roost, where could the dunlins find safety after all of the intertidal zone in Boundary Bay had been inundated? This question has vital implications for shorebirds anywhere on tide water! In other coastal regions, they retreat to some bare ground that remains above water even during the highest tides. In Washington State, as noted by Joseph Buchanan, dunlins move to wave-swept beaches that can be as far as eight miles (15 km) away from their estuarine feeding grounds. In Holland, hundreds of thousands of wintering shorebirds collect at high tide on traditional refuges such as sandbars about five miles (8 km) away from their feeding grounds. At other sites, shorebirds commute shorter distances and fly to inland fields. This is, to some extent, the case at Boundary Bay. Canadian Wildlife Service biologist Dr. Robert Butler and his colleagues have counted as many as thirteen thousand dunlins sitting out the tide on bare fields and wet meadows in the Fraser Delta of which Boundary Bay is an integral part. In addition, thousands of other dunlins, as noted by birdwatcher Richard Swanston, collect on the stone breakwaters that protect the Vancouver Island ferry landing. It is intriguing to realize that the opportunity to roost on fields and manmade jetties is an artifact of relatively recent times. The Fraser Delta was diked and drained for agriculture less than a century ago. The ferry landing was constructed even more recently. Prior to that time, all of the delta must have been covered with saltmarsh vegetation. Where did the dunlins go then after all open ground had been flooded by the high tides? The answer can still be learned today. During January, when daytime tides reach peak levels and inundate all mudflats including most of the saltmarsh, it is fascinating to see how the dunlins react! As the water rises and begins to lap at their bellies, the twittering little birds mass together on bits of wrack and tussocks on the edge of the saltmarsh. Standing shoulder to shoulder, a few snoozing with their head tucked in their feathers, they rest fitfully until sooner or later they get a rude awakening.

One day, I was sitting on the dike near a huge, densely packed flock of dunlins, a silver mat on the saltgrass, when an adult tiercel, coming from inland, shot by at arm's length. Streaking over the top of the dike, he slammed headlong into a wall of rising birds, vanishing completely among them. He reappeared moments later with a prey in his feet. In this same way, roosting dunlins were harassed by the sneaky merlin. Even harriers tried again and again, terrorizing the flocks, although they seldom succeeded in catching something. Getting out of the way only as far as necessary, the dunlins landed again after the bothersome hawk had passed. However, it took only one attack by a falcon to make the dunlins abandon the shore. Some flocks went inland, particularly if the fields were waterlogged by heavy rain. But most dunlins sought refuge in their wings, far out over the ocean! That's where they stayed, remaining airborne for as long as it took for the tide to turn! This over-ocean flocking behavior is an amazing, never-before-reported phenomenon, an antipredator strategy that I discovered by spending day after day on the dike from first light to dusk. During light breezes, the flocks cruised high in the sky. Strong winds or rain caused them to stay low in the trough of the waves. Flapping their wings slowly, the birds exerted themselves as little as possible, floating on the turbulent air and making little headway against the wind. No doubt, this over-ocean flocking was costly in terms of energy. Instead of resting, the flocks remained airborne for three or four hours, depending on the height of the tide. When they finally returned to shore, they touched down tentatively on the edge of the saltmarsh, but one attack by a falcon could send them back up for another spell. Until, at last, the waters began to ebb and the birds spread out over the shallows.

Dutch ornithologists, such as Dr. Theunis Piersma, have calculated that flights between mudflat and roost over the Waddenzee come at a significant metabolic cost, draining 10 percent of their fat reserves. By comparison, the dunlins of Boundary Bay must spend even more energy by staying aloft for several hours. I reckon that they can only afford this extravagant high-tide intermezzo if the local food supply is very abundant. This is apparently the case as divulged by studies of the marine organisms present in the mud and shallows of the estuary. Boundary Bay is one the most productive shorebird feeding grounds on the Pacific Coast. A fair question is: would these dunlins elect to sit out high tide on the ground if suitable open ground were available? I am sure they would. During a few days of extreme cold when the bay was frozen over as far as the eye could see, I saw no high-tide flocking. Small flocks of dunlins that had remained in the area roosted on the ice far from shore. Others stayed in a spot of saltmarsh sparsely covered with vegetation. Instead of resting, these birds continued to search for food on the frozen mud. As soon as the tide dropped, they flew out over the mud and fed ravenously. It was also revealing to see that their reaction to falcons was now far less intense than usual. Instead of drawing together in dense flocks high in the sky, only those dunlins directly in line with the falcon got out of the way and they landed immediately afterwards near the same place! Also here, as it had been for the ducks on Vancouver Island, the need to eat and the need to avoid predation are a trade-off. These dunlins were starving and had no energy to waste on antipredator exercises, at least no more than absolutely necessary. It was also an eye-opener for me to return to the bay in April. At that time, daytime high tides were about three feet (1 m) lower than in January and I saw no over-ocean flocking. As the waters crested, a wide strip of mudflat remained dry, allowing the dunlins to roost or keep feeding well away from the saltmarsh. Midwinter here is obviously the critical period. Although the nighttime cycle stays lower, the extremely high daytime tides force the dunlins to seek refuge in the only open place available, the sky. And each time it is a fantastic sight to watch them take to the air, not only because of the impressive flight maneuvers in themselves, but because even then some of their enemies cannot leave them alone.

Suspended on the wind, far out over the stormy ocean, twenty or thirty thousand dunlins float slowly back and forth in long, wavering streams, like veils of fog. Suddenly they draw together, congealing into a giant serpent, undulating low over the waves, shaking in terror. Portions break away and balloon into the sky, alternately flashing silver and black. Among them, a black trident rises and falls in vertical zigzags, a serration of violent stoops and ascensions. Gradually, the panic subsides. The dunlins spread out again and resume their solemn cruising, their immense number reduced by one. It is the price they pay, in flesh and blood, that keeps the peregrine on the wing. And all we humans can do is watch and enjoy in awe and admiration.

Foot note: The above interaction between peregrines, bald eagles, dunlins and ducks were typical of January conditions. During November of 1998, I found dunlins about as numerous as usual. However, waterfowl were more abundant, particularly teal, and bald eagles were scarce! Apparently, most arrive later after salmon spawning runs in northern rivers are finished. The few eagles that did frequent the bay in November hunted waterfowl and were keen on taking advantage of peregrines, even shadowing them in flight, ready to pounce on downed ducks. Apparently, later in winter, after a cold spell, a portion of the waterfowl leaves, perhaps to be followed by some of the duck-hunting peregrines. Those that remain concentrate on dunlins, which can be carried out of reach of the increasingly abundant eagles.

Chapter 13

Peregrines and People

Birds of prey have been venerated by humans since antiquity, although their significance was largely spiritual as heraldic totems or mythical messengers of the Gods. The practical use of raptorial birds dates back at least four thousand years and began in Asia. It involved the training of hawks and falcons as winged allies of human hunters, primarily as a means of capturing wild meat for the table. During the Middle Ages, returning crusaders introduced falconry to Europe where it became the Sport of Kings, a fashionable pastime that lasted for centuries. From Austria to Britain, the care and training of captive raptors pervaded everyday life for a wide array of citizens, who took their prized hunters along to all social functions, including church. References to hawks and hawking featured prominently in the English literature of the time. Shakespeare frequently used birding terms and analogies that are still in common use today. Words such as "coward" and "haggard" were derived from falconry. So are the expressions "in a towering rage," "taken by surprise," "beat around the bush" and "as vulnerable as a sitting duck." The meaning of these phrases may have widened but was originally restricted to the interaction of raptors and their prey.

The invention of the shotgun eventually ended the main reasons for flying falcons, but the practice has enjoyed a strong resurgence in recent times. Today there are thousands of devotees in the U.S.A. and Canada, as well as in Europe and Asia. How does falconry actually work? How do humans manage to control and cooperate with these wild and fiercely independent creatures?

There was a time, long ago, when I toyed with the idea of becoming a falconer myself. However, if you want to do justice to the bird, its care becomes an obsession and a way of life, requiring complete dedication as well as a practical, energetic personality. To those who have read the preceding chapters, it should be plain that I am the contemplative sort, content to sit on a stone or a log, with the sun at my back, enjoying the subtle intrigues of nature in their purest form. I for one would make a poor falconer. Watching wild falcons is much easier on me!

Lacking personal involvement with falconry, I can only give a viewpoint distilled from reading some of the classical books on the sport and inspired by a few field trips I had the pleasure of making with Henk Dijkstra, one of Holland's most experienced practitioners. Unfortunately, elsewhere I saw some of the negative aspects of this hobby when rare and treasured falcons fell into the hands of charlatans and ended up as mere lawn ornaments. This has nothing to do with falconry.

A falcon on the fist

At its best, the sport, or art form as some prefer to call it, is still conducted today the way it was centuries ago with a minimum of equipment that is still of the same basic design. In a sense, the captive falcon is controlled by its stomach. Taken from the wild when young, or obtained from captive breeding facilities, the bird is habituated to people until it is docile enough to sit on a gloved hand and accept food from its trainer. Its first flights from perching block to fist are short and secured by a line. Eventually, the falcon is allowed to fly free, but only if it is hungry, so that it can be expected to return quickly if offered a piece of meat. Traditionally, the food is tied onto a lure, a leather disk or a facsimile of a bird carcass attached to a string that can be swung around overhead or thrown into the air, making it visible from afar. The lure is weighted down with wood or metal, preventing the bird from carrying it away after "capture." When it is fully trained, a falcon is released only after suitable game has been spotted. The intended quarry can be a covey of partridges in a field or ducks swimming on a pond. As long as their enemy is above them in the air, waiting on, the partridges hide motionlessly in the stubble and do not dare to flee. Ducks stay safely on the water. To give the falcon a sporting chance, its handlers, shouting and waving arms, run up to flush the prey. Often the job is done by a spaniel or other hunting dog that has been waiting eagerly for the signal to rush in. The moment of truth arrives as soon as the quarry is airborne and the falcon makes its move, stooping to overtake and strike its target before it reaches cover. To create the best opportunity for a kill, the falconer endeavors to flush the quarry over open terrain at the right moment, when the circling falcon comes into a favorable position for attack.

The successful falcon, standing on its catch, should allow its master to approach and kneel down at its side. Offered a bit of fresh meat, the bird is enticed to step over onto the gloved hand to be secured by the short leather jesses attached to its legs. The quarry is spirited out of sight into the game bag. If worked with skill, a well-trained falcon can capture a succession of prey. However, it is not always easy to locate suitable targets and sometimes the quarry escapes. It is critical that the falcon recognizes the trainer as a provider of food, so that it can be called down to the lure or padded glove, to be rewarded with a bite to eat. As extra insurance that the bird can be retrieved even if it has flown out of sight, modern falconers equip it with a miniature radio-transmitter attached to a leg or a tail feather. At the end of the day, the precious hunter is taken home again, until the next field outing. To keep them in good physical shape, falcons should be flown every day, a demanding task for practitioners who live in the big city.

From the start, to do justice to the bird, falconry requires dedication and infinite patience. Many followers are lifelong devotees who see their hobby as an advanced form of birdwatching. It is no doubt thrilling and the culmination of much effort to see a well-trained falcon capture its prey. The victories are all the more sweet because they come at a certain risk. Captives may become lost or die prematurely as a result of disease or accident, a heartbreaking end to the dream, forcing the falconer to begin the long training process all over again with another bird.

If you wish to see a peregrine in action and do not want the bother of keeping one yourself, you might like to accompany a practicing falconer. Enthusiastic field assistants are usually welcome and needed. Failing that opportunity, your only chance lies in watching the wild ones. Even then, with luck, you might have some falconry-style fun without its obligations! If hungry, a wild raptor can be quick to take advantage of your services as a beater. As described in chapter nine, wintering peregrines, as well as gyrfalcons, eagerly pursued ducks that I scared up out of a pond or ditch, either involuntarily or on purpose! In the same way, on my walks over the pastures around Beaverhills Lake, I have been followed by merlins keen on dashing after sparrows that I happened to flush out of the grass. In wilderness regions, birds of prey, such as goshawks that may never have seen a human being before, do not hesitate to kill prey right in front of you. From the beginning, falconry was a very simple and natural alliance. In a way, it was the hawk that gave people the idea and taught them the tricks of the game! Even the fact that its quarry is taken away by the falconer is not necessarily unnatural; wild falcons are quite used to being robbed by larger raptors such as eagles. Following the loss of its prey, the hungry falcon is almost immediately ready to hunt again.

Nowadays, falconry comes with some strings attached, so to speak. In most jurisdictions, the keeping of hawks is regulated by a permit system intended to curtail unauthorized and irresponsible excesses. Moreover, novices are often supervised by experienced instructors who instill a sense of responsibility for the welfare of the captives. Getting together with like-minded people to exchange ideas and adventures is all part of the lure and enjoyment of this ancient sport, which always was and still is very much a social activity, quite in contrast to watching the wild ones.

Bred in a barn

Falconers, along with everyone else interested in wildlife and birds of prey, got a very hardhitting message during the critical 1960s, when peregrine populations plummeted through the insidious side-effects of toxic chemicals used in agriculture. Many people thought that falcons and other raptors were on the way toward extinction. As a consequence, the demand for captive peregrines skyrocketed. At the same time, this crisis became the falconer's finest hour. The best of them got together and used their knowledge and skill to induce this beloved raptor to breed in captivity, not only to secure the future of falconry, but also to eventually rebuild wild populations. This effort devoted to a single species is without parallel in the world. And so is its unqualified success! To the falconers involved, their triumph is particularly rewarding since it was seriously doubted by many, including me, that a highflying avian hunter like the peregrine could be coaxed into laying eggs and raising young inside a barn! Yet, it became a successful routine after a score of technical problems had been worked out.

The first large-scale attempts to propagate falcons in captivity began in Canada and the U.S.A. in the early 1970s. Young were produced in 1973 and 1974 at two major facilities: Cornell University in New York State and the Canadian Wildlife Service breeding center at Wainwright, Alberta. Prior to that time, several private individuals, such as Canadians Frank Beebe and David Hancock, had experimented and achieved success on a minor scale. There were others in the U.S.A. Incidentally, the very first one to succeed, more than two decades earlier, had been a German falconer. In North America, the total number of breeding facilities soon exceeded two dozen and by 1980 their combined output had reached several hundred peregrines per year.

The first captive-raised juveniles were released into the wild in 1975 through an ancient falconry technique called hacking. The young, still in the downy stage and four to five weeks old, were at first confined to an open-fronted box secured on a cliff or to the side of a building. They were fed daily with dead, farm-raised quail dropped down through a chute, while the human provider stayed out of view. When the falcons were about six weeks old and their flight feathers had almost fully developed, the wooden bars on the front of the cage were lifted, allowing the young to step outside onto a platform giving a view of the wide world below and the sky above. One after the other, the fledglings took off on their hazardous maiden flight. Upon return to the cage, they would find food for several more weeks. Meanwhile, the birds had the opportunity to become self-sufficient. Guided by instinct, they learned to hunt all on their own, improving their skill through practice.

As more and more survivors of the ambitious program settled down to nest in the wild at numerous sites across the continent, releases were scaled down or stopped. In Alberta and Ontario the last mass releases occurred in 1996, the same year that the

Wainwright breeding facility was finally closed. In total, more than 6,000 young falcons were let go into the wild: 2,722 in the American West, 729 in the Midwest, 1,229 in the East, and just more than 1,500 in Canada.

Simultaneously with the start of the captive breeding effort, there had been victories in the battle against the use of toxic chemicals. Between 1969 and 1972, DDT was banned or greatly restricted in the U.S.A. and Canada. That slowly translated into renewed reproductive success of the birds of prey. By 1994, the North American peregrine population had increased spectacularly since the great decline in the 1960s. As estimated by Dr. James Enderson *et al.* and extrapolated from known surveys, the 1994 continental breeding population was believed to be some 7,000 pairs, including 4,400 in Canada, 2,100 in U.S.A., 450 in Greenland, and 170 in Mexico. Added to the nonbreeding segment of the population, including the young, the total number of peregrines on this continent might conservatively be calculated at twenty to twenty-five thousand birds.

Lure of the city

A remarkable phenomenon during the peregrine's return has been its adoption of urban environments. Prior to the 1960s, there had been a few records of falcons breeding in cities such as Montreal and New York. In Spain, falcons nest on the ruins of castles. In Holland and Germany, wintering falcons commonly use church steeples as hunting perches. However, during the 1980s, peregrines released in North America settled to nest on downtown highrises all across the United States and Canada. As of 1997, there are pairs breeding in more than sixty cities. In addition to these urban nesters, other pairs found a niche on prosaic, noisy and cluttered edifices such as river bridges, power generating stations, cement plants and oil refineries. In the American Midwest, 75 percent of peregrines now nest on manmade structures. Some of these birds had been captive-raised and released in the same area. But they often attracted partners from distant points of release, even from the wild, as evidenced by numbered leg bands or their absence.

The reason why cities and industrial sites are attractive to peregrines is basic. First of all, tall buildings look like super cliffs, ideal as hunting perches. Secondly, pigeons that abound in railyards and city parks constitute a reliable, year-round prey. They can be particularly important in the Canadian north where migratory song birds and waterfowl do not arrive until late April or May. In prairie cities such as Winnipeg, Saskatoon and Calgary, the first peregrines return already in March, competing with each other for urban territories while the surrounding countryside is still frozen solid. At this time of year, pigeons are practically the only prey, a steady source of food that even tempts the odd falcon to stay all winter. In the past, breeding populations at this latitude were highly migratory, departing in early fall and returning six months later.

The productivity of city nests appears to be quite comparable to wild sites. The sad fact is that a number of fledglings as well as adults come to grief after hitting powerlines and windows. On the other hand, the falcon's most serious natural enemy, the great-horned owl, is usually absent. Moreover, a nesting ledge on a city highrise is generally safe from two-legged raiders and vandals.

Although the heart of Seattle, New York or Edmonton may not be the most inspiring environment in the world to watch a peregrine, its adoption of the big city is a tribute to its rugged adaptability and a feather in the cap of all those who have striven toward its preservation. Barring a repeat of the pesticide era or a worse human-created catastrophe, I have no doubt that the resilient bolt from the blue will outlive us all.

Chapter 14

Powerplant Episode

In 1995, fourteen years after the first peregrines began to colonize cities in western Canada, one of their offspring got together with a male of unknown origin and nested on a powerplant by Wabamun Lake in central Alberta. This happy union followed an initiative by the Alberta Falconers' Association. Their members, with the cooperation of TransAlta Utilities, had installed a wooden nest box high on the smoke stack. The falcons took to it like ducks to water. A few years later, there were pairs nesting on three of four coal-burning generating stations, no more than a few miles apart.

It may seem almost unbelievable that a lofty raptor such as the peregrine, this exquisite jewel in the crown of avian evolution, should deign to establish its eyrie on a powerplant, one of the largest and perhaps most intrusive structures to clutter today's landscape. How can this high-strung creature cope with the disturbance and hazards surrounding the plant? The answer came to me during a visit to Langara Island off the northwest Pacific Coast. One breezy afternoon, two juvenile falcons were perched on an offshore rock washed by the heaving ocean. As the tide rose, one of the birds left, perhaps after it had been hit by spray flung up by the fury of wind and waves. The falcon flew to the giant conifers on shore, maneuvering to find a new perch between the tangled branches and spiky snags. It suddenly struck me that there may not be that much difference, from a falcon's perspective, between the imposing wall of a Pacific rain forest and a powerplant surrounded by its jungle of pylons and poles! As well, the throb of generators may not be louder than the roar of wind and the ceaseless crashing of ocean surf.

As mentioned in the previous chapter, a tall building such as a powerplant provides the peregrine with two strategic advantages.

Firstly, it presents a prominent perch overlooking an area abounding in prey. Secondly, the nest is out of reach of potential enemies. Another plus point is that the huge building functions like a four-sided cliff, creating an updraft by any wind direction, giving just-fledged juveniles a lift during the critical time when they launch their maiden flight. Moreover, at the Wabamun plant the flat gravel-topped roof of the powerhouse, right below the three smoke stacks, served as a safe landing pad. All in all, the place has proven to be a haven for falcon families ever since they first adopted it.

The peregrines even took advantage of the foul exhaust of the plant! Soaring in the column of rising vapor, they gained height very quickly! On overcast and rainy days, when soaring flight was not possible, the stacks made convenient vantage points. Perched on the railing of the catwalk near the very top, they were like pirates lying in wait for unsuspecting victims. The powerplant pair presented me with a convenient opportunity to watch breeding peregrines hunt right from their nest site. I had not enjoyed such a classic setup since 1978 when I spent a few days at a cliff eyrie on Lake Athabasca.

Magic moments

By the time of my first visits to the lake, in 1997, Wabamun had become a meeting place of peregrines from several origins, including unbanded birds and black-banded city-bred birds from as far away as Winnipeg and Calgary. In 1998, the male at the powerplant where I watched had been replaced with a red-banded, captive-raised individual probably released on the Red Deer River. That summer, I went there three or four days each week from late July to the end of August, less often thereafter. These were by no means the most serene and relaxing hours I ever spent looking for falcons. On the contrary! My tolerance for noise and traffic is far less than theirs. Particularly when no peregrines were in sight or if they did nothing more than perch for hours on end, I would soon get tired of the roar of generators and the rumble of trains and trucks passing by. Another drawback that often taxed my limit was the scorching sun. Watching peregrines during the heat of summer was a new experience for me. If I sought shade, my field of view in these industrial surroundings became even more restricted. Losing sight of the falcon, disappearing behind buildings or trees soon after it had taken off at hunting speed, was a frustrating but common scenario, even if I watched from an open point about half a mile (0.8 km) away from the plant. A lot of hunting action went in the other direction, but sometimes I happened to be in the right spot at the right time. As everywhere, seeing something of interest was ultimately a matter of chance, regardless of patience and endurance.

There did not seem to be any set pattern to the pair's activities. No two days were the same. The adults might bring prey to the young at any time during the afternoon or evening. I do not know what went on at day break. I suspect they did little hunting then if they had entered the night with a full crop of food. On a few days when I did make a special effort to be there early, an hour or so after sunrise, nothing happened until hours later. One clear and warm morning, I watched the tiercel from eight o'clock until one. All he did was sit on his metal throne, a power pylon, overlooking the shoreline marshes. Snoozing, he frequently closed his eyes for a minute at a time. Around noon, after an extensive spell of preening, he made just one very brief flight to switch to a spot a little lower in the pylon where an overhead beam cast a bit of shade! During the same morning, the female had been resting for hours on the top railing of the smoke stack within sight of the tiercel. She too sought shade later on.

I seldom stayed longer than four or five hours, usually in late afternoon and evening, and I was content if the day's boredom was relieved with one or two interesting episodes. Over the course of two months, they added up to an intimate glimpse into the magic of this happy family.

Fun and games

Since the nest box was too high above ground to look into, I saw nothing of the young until they were close to fledging. The first chick, a dapper tiercel, emerged on July 22. He waddled about on the circular catwalk adjacent to the nest box and flexed his wings, as if he were impatient to leave. His dad seemed to know exactly what was going on. Arriving with a small prey, he touched down in front of the juvenile on the very edge of the platform, but he veered away again at once. He did this three times in a row. Twice he dropped the item, recovering it quickly after a vertical stoop. Was he just clumsy? Or was he deliberately teasing and enticing the youngster to follow him in flight? After his third attempt, the male gave up and instead made a perfect food transfer to another youngster standing in the entrance of the nest box!

On July 24, two of the young, both tiercels, had fledged. Their lone sister was still in the box. From time to time, she flapped her broad wings and gazed keenly down on her siblings fluttering over the flat roof below. Three days later, she too was airborne. The tiercels flew circles around her, striking and grabbing at her wings and tail. In defense, she slashed back. Considering their razor-sharp talons, it seemed amazing that these playful scraps did not result in injury. They all survived unscathed, or so it seemed to me.

The tiercels' progress was astounding. Four or five days after fledging, they soared and stooped with abandon, and they could make a perfect landing on any prominence they fancied. During the following week, the three began to spend more and more time away, having fun with swallows and harassing gulls. From time to time, I picked up a youngster in the glasses, soaring high over the plant and sailing off, wings swept back like a pro. Toward evening, all three returned home. They might even huddle together, preening each other's feathers or touching bills like courting pigeons.

Good times for all

As the trio became more mobile and confident, they explored the surroundings, pausing for brief rests on spruce trees, poles or open ground. They also idled away hours high in the sky, careening and tumbling together, until hunger forced them back to earth. If they spotted mother sitting quietly on the smoke stack, they wailed at her: "Go get us some food!"

At this eyrie, the female took an active part in supplying the young, but she satisfied her own needs first. After a long absence she might return with a full crop but without bringing anything for the fledglings. At other times, she tossed the half-eaten carcass of a gull or duck on the catwalk, or allowed a juvenile to take the prey from her feet while she remained airborne.

Although the male stayed away much of the time, probably to avoid his pushy progeny, he did most of the foraging and obviously delighted in the task. One evening, he arrived with a shorebird, yellow legs dangling. Landing on a nearby pylon, he looked keenly about, expecting his kids, but none were to be seen. A minute later, taking his prey along, he described a half circle around the chimneys. Very soon, all three young showed up in pursuit. As one of them came up from behind and below, the male exchanged the food talon to talon. At other times when making a delivery, he stayed much higher, circling and waiting for the youngsters to climb toward him. The race might be won by a keen and alert tiercel, quick to snatch the prize out of dad's feet, but he lost it again as soon as big sister caught up. She just tore the item out of his grasp. She was equally aggressive if dad was unwilling to surrender a just-caught bird, perhaps because he wanted to eat part of it himself first. Chasing and accosting him, she slashed upward until he dropped his prey. She always ended up getting the lion's share of the food, while her little brothers were left hungry and had to wait their turn or fend for themselves.

No doubt the youngsters knew exactly how their food was obtained. With eyes sharper than mine they watched their parents. One day I arrived just in time to see the adult female hurriedly leave the smoke stack, straight as a speeding arrow, and intercept a small duck flying over the woods toward the lake. Turning back with the quarry in her clutches, she was pursued by the two young tiercels. One of them grabbed hold of the duck and hung upside down for a few seconds, until she shook him off. She alighted on a pylon, her usual plucking post, and began to crop, flanked by both kids, begging and screaming. One gave up and left. The other tried to reach the food or take morsels from her bill. Eventually, nearly sated, she fed him a few bites, beak to beak, and allowed him to snatch a severed wing. This happened on the eighth or ninth day after fledging.

The female consumed the entire duck, a bufflehead, the smallest of our waterfowl. (To my surprise, she also swallowed the long intestine, something I had never noticed before although this may well be common.)

On another occasion, when the female had killed a much larger duck, all three youngsters took turns at the carcass lying on some open ground by the settling ponds behind the plant. This spot was out of bounds to the public, so I was unable to check the species of duck. As it happened, just prior to the time when this kill must have been made, I had (deliberately) flushed a mixed group of teal and mallards from the pond in the hope the falcon, sitting on the smoke stack in the distance, would show up in pursuit. When the ducks separated, I kept the glasses trained on the teal which returned to the pond unharmed. I should have followed the mallards instead! They had flown toward the area I had come from. A while later when I walked back over the dike, I discovered the juvenile female on the carcass of a large duck. The young tiercels sat on the ground nearby. Mother was perched on a post and boldly approached me, protesting loudly and looking me over with suspicion. (I am sure this was not her way of saying thanks for flushing the mallards!)

Another day she landed on a pylon with a just-caught Franklin's gull. She did not get much time to eat. Minutes later, her three kids arrived, screaming and jostling for space on the narrow beams. One of the tiercels got so excited he alighted on mother's back! Crowded off her perch, she took her prey and left, pursued by the youngsters, all of them disappearing from sight behind some trees. Presently, I found the juveniles on the flat roof of a shed, the female feeding on the gull, her brothers watching. Mother was sitting on a pole nearby. When I quickly moved in to examine the prey, she cacked and circled toward me, then returned to her guard post. A while later, she fiercely attacked a goshawk which retreated to the woods in a hurry. I had seen her mess with this big female gos before and I was surprised by the peregrine's ferocity. She had almost tackled her dangerous antagonist, while two of the juveniles had joined her in the rout! Recognizing their enemies, the youngsters were also quick to harass the local red-tail, taking care to stay out of reach of its claws as the big but slow hawk rolled to ward off the swooping pests.

Hunting together

As early as August 11, the youngsters began to attack prey on their own. They pursued blackbirds low over the ground or swooped at passerines and shorebirds high in the sky. Especially the tiercels demonstrated fantastic powers of acceleration, but they were quickly outmaneuvered. Tiring of their efforts, they returned to the plant and wailed at their parents.

One area of adult-juvenile interaction about which I had hoped to learn more was group hunting. After a few weeks it became routine. The first episode literally fell out of the blue sky as I sat quietly on the dike by the settling ponds. The young female was perched on the opposite side. Suddenly, with an anxious scream, a Franklin's gull splashed down into the water between us. An adult falcon shot by overhead! Instantly, the juvenile sprang into the air and began a series of eager but futile swoops at the gull, which managed to defuse every attack by splashing aside.

In the meantime, the adult had disappeared. Scanning the cloud-studded skies, I first picked up the tiercel, and as their soaring circles converged, his mate. Presently, she zoomed down in a terrific stoop at another gull flying at some height over the ponds. The tiercel followed. Narrowly dodging one or two repeat passes, the desperate gull plunged into the water, and in seconds it was swooped at by five falcons including the three juveniles! Again, the upshot was that the gull dodged all of them and eventually it was left alone.

In ensuing weeks, I saw a lot more family fun. Each evening, the youngsters waited for the adult tiercel to show up at the plant and begin a bout of foraging. They soared up with him as he gained

height over the smoke stacks, looking for prey. One day, he launched a terrific stoop far out over the lake aimed at a small shorebird. He missed and seconds later all three juveniles were hotly pursuing the same target! But none were successful.

Flying back to the plant, the tiercel regained altitude and presently made another attack over the lake, where he scattered a flock of blackbirds. Once more all three youngsters joined the party, each pursuing a different target. With four falcons swirling across the sky in several directions, I had a tough time deciding which one to follow. However, it soon became clear that none of them had managed to affect a capture. On the way back to the plant, even though he was not carrying any food, dad was hassled mercilessly by the young female, as if she was giving him a hard time for not coming through with the goodies. In subsequent, more successful group hunts, she took the prey from him at once.

August 25 was a highlight when I saw for the first time that the quarry was caught by a juvenile, albeit with dad's help! This cooperative effort had been started by the young female. Giving dad a not-so-subtle hint that she was hungry, she had pushed him off his pylon where he had been preening for more than an hour. He left at once and soared up to a great height, joined by two juveniles. Both played around together and harassed dad mercilessly, but they broke off their games at once as soon as he got serious. He made several futile attacks that carried him out of view, each time returning to

soar over the plant. At last, he set course for the lake, passing high overhead in a mile-long stoop, terminating in a vertical plunge aimed at one of three small ducks. They dodged narrowly. Failing again in his second stoop, the tiercel seemed to hesitate, positioning himself for a third stoop, but before he got a chance the juvenile female slanted down out of the blue. She seized the quarry without a hitch and carried it back to the plant.

August 26 was again a red-letter day when the tiercel seized and released a passerine for his juvenile partners! The small bird dropped a few feet, then flew on, to be stooped at by a young male. He failed to catch it and dad repeated the procedure with the same result. Pressing on after the falling prey, all of them disappeared below the tree line. When they came back into view, the adult was carrying the item, which was quickly expropriated by a juvenile tiercel. Within the next half hour, I saw two similar hunts in which the adult caught and released a small songbird, which was then snapped up by a juvenile. All three of these spectacular, classical group hunts had involved multiple stoops and swoops, as well as a long descent from a great height!

Parental guidance

How would it end? Would the adults, sooner or later, get enough of their demanding youngsters and drive them out of their territory? This might make sense on the west coast, where breeding peregrines occupy eyrie cliffs all year. However, not so in central Alberta. The powerplant pair, instead of chasing their young away, allowed them to come and go as they pleased. However, by the same token, they might leave themselves. The nesting cycle was only a passing episode in the nomadic existence of these highly migratory creatures. The continent was their domain.

The adult female's presence was infrequent. By late afternoon, she had usually stuffed herself on a gull or duck, and she sat the rest of the day on a pole away from the plant. But her mate kept up doing his duty, assisting her in attacks on prey, and later supplying the young. Diligent and tireless, he spent two or three hours each evening hunting with them, first satisfying his demanding daughter, which grabbed the food he brought even though she had just eaten, then her brothers. By sundown, after a brief rest, he began to look for his own meal.

By early September, the family was still together and the young seemed better behaved, less dependent. They allowed the parents to spend more time with them in peace and harmony. Sometimes all five of them soared together and their interaction as a hunting group had entered another stage. Dad seemed to know exactly what his kids needed. He guided them along with skill and patience. For me as the human observer, it was easy to fall into the trap of anthropomorphism. But the facts spoke for themselves. Consider the following sequence of events, which took place on the warm and clear evening of September 3.

In late afternoon, two of the youngsters, brother and sister, had been fooling around over the plant, until they suddenly took off to meet the approaching adult tiercel. He was carrying a small bird in his bill, a present for his kids, dropped in midair. It was quickly snatched up by the young tiercel, which soon lost it to the female. Nothing new here, except the fact that the adult was subsequently allowed to rest unmolested on the nest box.

After half an hour or so, he took off and began to soar, joined by the juveniles. Following the tiercel in the glasses, I watched him ascend in quick, wing-beating circles to intercept a gull. After two vicious stoops at the dodging target, high in the sky, he held off until the juvenile female arrived. Rushing down at her target, she pursued it out of sight beyond shoreline trees. Did the tiercel actually set up this gull as a suitable prey for his big daughter? I believe he did indeed, as he had done with the duck in the hunt of August 25. I think he understood the capacity and requirements of the female, and she in turn appeared to depend on him. Or so it seemed, as illustrated by the events of September 6.

In the late afternoon of this warm and breezy day, the juvenile female had chased blackbirds and other passerines without success, until she alighted on the highest perch above the plant. She was looking for the adult tiercel, and so was I! Close to an hour later, by sheer luck I picked him up, soaring. Waiting on, he cruised slowly upwind toward the lake, sailing on the lateral flow of air or beating his wings in a rowing rhythm. Far away, almost out of sight, he turned back downwind, to be cut off from my view behind some trees. In the meantime, the juvenile had gone. Oh well, just another opportunity lost, I thought.

By force of habit searching the sky through the glasses, I presently picked up two tiercels some distance away. They were in a hurry and heading in my direction. The adult was in the lead, climbing at full throttle, his wings a vibrant blur. The target, brightly white in the blue, turned out to be a Franklin's gull! Overhauled in seconds, it was driven down by the alternating tiercels, and just as it dropped from view below a dike, the juvenile female joined in for the kill. A few minutes later, peeking over the high ground, I found her on her victim. Little brother was sitting on a clump of earth close-by. Dad looked on from a powerpole, no doubt with pride in his dapper heart!

On his own, or with the young tiercels, the adult tiercel always selected smaller prey, such as shorebirds and passerines. Then too, I got the distinct impression that he set up the target for them, and desisted after one or two passes. The quarry was then followed down by the juveniles. If they made a catch, dad quickly departed. If he had managed to seize the prey himself, it was released forthwith, dead or alive.

Time and again, I watched the adult tiercel set out with both his sons. If one had been satisfied, prevailing over his jealous sibling, dad continued to hunt with the other. If he took a brief rest on the smoke stack, his eager partner waited nearby. Either one might decide to get going again. Almost a match in speed, the youngster, soaring with the adult, might even be first in selecting a target, with dad following and chaperoning the attack.

On their own

During the time when the young were keen to hunt in concert with their dad, they also initiated their own wide-ranging forays, alone or with siblings. One late evening, they rose over the plant together, swirling in fast circles and quickly ascending to the thermal summit. Suddenly one of the tiercels broke away, surging ahead with cleaving wings. He stooped far out over the lake, his aim a small shorebird. Seconds later the female plummeted passed him, but both failed to strike.

Returning to the plant, they soared again in unison, three minuscule black arrowheads drawing mesmerizing patterns on a luminous firmament. Then, beating steadily, the female took the lead, followed by one of the tiercels. Traveling toward the setting sun and passing very high overhead, they looked down on me and on their lakeside world of marshes and woods, any bird that moved at their command. A mile away, specks in the cloudless void, they fell like meteors, here one moment, gone the next.

The most amazing thing was that these youngsters hunted exactly like the adults. Had they been taught to do so? Yes and no. They had watched their parents, joined them and followed their example. Now they relied on their own unfailing talents and destiny to become nature's most perfect predator! The wonder of it all was that these birds had achieved this in so little time, less than three months after crawling out of the egg!

Aerial drama

Although the behavior of the young, their interaction with each other and with their parents had been fascinating to watch, the primary reason for my visits to the powerplant had been to study the hunting habits of these breeding adults. What I discovered, one episode at a time, turned out to be quite different from much that I had seen in other study areas, such as Beaverhills Lake and the Pacific Coast. There, migrating or wintering peregrines had aimed the vast majority of attacks on prey on the ground or in the water. By contrast, the powerplant birds appeared to be entirely oriented toward flying prey. This was a consequence of habitat. Here, there were no wide mudflats or open agricultural lands. The country surrounding the Wabamun industrial complex and the village by that name was mainly wooded, while the lake shore featured a margin of reedy shallows. Arching over it all was the great dome of summer sky, and this was the falcons' undisputed domain.

During suitable weather, their strategy was always the same. They soared up to an immense altitude before they began looking for prey. As they drifted back and forth over the area, it became increasingly difficult to keep them in focus, especially if they crossed the sun. Looking directly at the light through binoculars is said to cause blindness. So I took care to lower my eyes in time. Finding the tiny dot again on the other side of the glare was a great relief.

Idly soaring, or so it seemed, the hunting falcon might wait on for ten or twenty minutes. Then, it began to travel across the sky on a straight course, in a power glide or flapping its wings, faster and faster. The female's target was usually a gull, the slender Franklin's gull or the larger ring-bill. Avoiding the stoop, they responded to their peril in a characteristic way: shifting aside and towering back up much higher than before, like a tennis ball flung against the pavement. In some hunts, the action took place so far away the combatants faded from sight, dissolving into thin air. In others, the falcon either gave up soon or forced the screaming gull lower and lower until both dropped out of my sight behind trees and other obstructions. If the falcon emerged again and resumed soaring, I knew that the attack had failed. If she did not reappear, I sometimes checked out the area and found her standing on her prey.

Interestingly, nearly every time I saw the female go in for the attack, her mate showed up too. He suddenly streaked down from the heavens and stooped at the gull, alternating with his partner. If they failed to connect, the falcons resumed soaring together. Their circles widening, they separated and forced me to choose, but I am sure they kept an eye on each other. If I followed the tiercel in the glasses, he might take off suddenly to reunite with his partner, which was swooping at a gull or had just made a catch.

Tandem hunting, as some authors have termed this phenomenon, is common at breeding sites across the world, from Britain to North Africa, from Quebec to New York. In 1978, during my brief stay on Lake Athabasca, two of the three hunting flights I observed there had been cooperative efforts, of which one resulted in the kill of a nighthawk. The male had secured the prey at his first stoop but released it an instant later. Before the stunned nighthawk had dropped more than a few feet, it was clutched by the female.

This is exactly what happened one day when the powerplant pair stopped soaring and raced high over the lake, female in the lead. She was the first to stoop but missed. As she towered up for her next pass, the tiercel streaked down and seized the prey, a shorebird. He dropped it at her approach and she gathered the falling bundle up in her feet to take it back to the plant where she was eagerly welcomed by her daughter.

After the young had left, by the second week of September, the relationship of the adult pair bloomed all over again. It was plain that they were in tune with each other. Although they might spend much of the day apart, they came together toward evening. Perching in view of each other or while soaring, they were quick to spot the same target, a shorebird or passerine, a mile or more away. Racing in for the kill, they stooped alternately. If the male was first to capture the prey, she did not take it from him by force, but allowed him to eat undisturbed. Sitting on a pylon nearby, she waited for him to finish his meal. Then, they took off again without further delay, a deadly duo, the tiercel a little higher than his partner, their wings cleaving the air in unison with intense determination.

The upshot

On his own, the powerplant tiercel hunted a range of birds, but mostly small passerines. He made his choice circling in a sky which seemed totally empty to me. One evening, early on during my observations, I kept him in the glasses for nearly an hour. The low sun was veiled behind a band of crimson cloud. Sharply etched against the bright western light, the tiny spearpoint of the tiercel was relatively easy to follow, despite the great distance and height. He might have been close to a mile high. Reaching the limit of thermal lift, he boosted his circling speed with spells of flapping. Six times I saw him attack.

Sighting prey in the distance, he took off with a burst of wing beats, then descended in a shallow parabola curving down into the vertical, tearing the sky. Once he fragmented a small group of finches that exploded outward like splinters off a cutting block. The other times I caught a momentary glimpse of a small songbird, jinking aside. Ricochetting back up, the tiercel looped around for a second or third stoop as the target plummeted to earth, but he failed each time and resumed soaring.

After another attack, hurtling earthward deeply, he had lost most of his altitude and returned to the smoke stacks to regain his pitch.

At last, very high, shimmering in the hot vapor, he drew his circles right overhead. It had become progressively more difficult to keep him in my shaking glasses. Now, bending over backwards, reluctant to let go, it became agony, forcing me to turn around. Lost him!

Scanning the sky slowly and methodically, I found him again, the merest speck of dust, far away. Then, he turned and hurried back, flicking his wings in quick bursts close to the tail. Tucking them in tightly, he keeled over and fell perpendicularly for hundreds of feet, a teardrop of shining gold lit by the sun. Missed! Throwing up, he slammed down and up again three or four times in a frenzy of violence, his target a small passerine. It was absolutely amazing to see how well the little bird coped with its peril, twisting aside erratically, plunging deep down, the tiercel right on its tail, until the two merged into one....

After delivering his still-warm offering at the plant, the tiercel boosted his altitude over the stacks, rocking in the gusty exhaust. He stayed in the rising mist for a long time, mounting ever higher, a minuscule, vibrating blur. When he finally set his course, beating his wings decisively, he darted out over the lake, a flickering dot melting away in the glow of sundown, becoming one with the sky.

I could finally rest my aching arms and catch my breath. What a show it had been! Over the years, in scenic settings of prairie and ocean, I have often thought that I had seen the best of the peregrine. But here, in these prosaic surroundings, I had met a world-class champion. Riding the wind high over the plant, he and his mate transcended the affairs of mankind, taking their beauty and brilliance into the sky.

It may seem folly to try to express the high drama that had unfolded here in mere figures. Yet, I had always wanted a chance to compare the hunting success rate of breeding peregrines to those of migrating and wintering falcons. By the time the summer ended, I had seen well over two hundred flights and deep stoops. The outcomes of 108 hunts were known and included twenty-three kills. This translates into a success rate of 21.3 percent, which is more than double the figures recorded at Beaverhills Lake and Boundary Bay.

This red-banded tiercel, captive-bred and released from a hacksite, was certainly an outstanding performer, maybe the greatest hunter I had ever seen! Admittedly, his actual score varied quite a bit. Once I saw him catch two prey in ten minutes. Another time, he came back with four passerines and two shorebirds in little over an hour. By the same token, he might catch nothing in a dozen terrific stoops. In a statistical sense these differences do not seem significant, just the law of averages, unless there were other factors at play as well, such as intent.

Obviously, his chances for success varied with his choice of target. To me, it seemed silly to stoop head-on at a flock of warblers low over the trees, like trying to hit butterflies with a bow and arrow. Yet, even then he sometimes succeeded, obliterating the tiny bird—a candle snuffed out by a gust of wind. As peregrines so often are, this tiercel was highly overpowered. Supercharged, he was a bullet with wings, hissing down from 3,000 feet upon a warbler or finch flitting lightly and erratically upon the air. Rocking aside in the draft of his terrifying stoop, the tiny bird plummeted headlong toward the safety of trees or bushes. The tiercel might give up after one or two passes. At other times, he was as agile as a merlin, swooping and swerving feverishly, following the plunging and side-slipping target right down to the ground.

Perhaps we must try to think like a peregrine. You win some, you lose some. Why should this tiercel score any higher than one kill out of five tries? He was undoubtedly a great provider, there were plenty of birds in the sky, and he had all the time in the world. What else was there to do? Sit on his pylon and preen his precious feathers? He was as good as he wanted to be. He certainly did not, as I did, keep a tally of hits and misses. A mere list of cyphers seems meaningful only to us. If this accomplished tiercel really wanted to kill, I am sure he would execute the task without much fuss at all, coolly biding his chance. This is the way I had come to know his kind in half a dozen different environments where I have had the privilege of watching the fabulous bolt from the blue.

Epilogue

The saga continues

Do we know all there is to know about peregrines? Tentatively, an affirmative conclusion might seem justified based on the enormous amount of information available today on this high-profile and much-studied species. However, all too often, long-term observation leads to insights that contradict established wisdom or myth. Even today, after spending a lifetime of watching wild peregrines, I still see behavior I have not seen before, occasionally forcing me to change my thinking on some detail of this multifaceted subject. In principle, it is best to record only one's actual observations, just the facts, without making them into a general rule about what falcons do and what they do not do. The peregrine is a highly individualistic and adaptable predator. No two behave exactly alike.

This overriding truth strikes me afresh each time I start looking at falcons in an environment new to me. As conveyed by the foregoing chapters, I have intensely studied their hunting habits in several, widely differing localities. Each time, the story turned out to be unique. However, it is just possible that I have seen no more than a portion of the peregrine's total repertoire, considering that my study areas were all situated in southern Canada, between five degrees of latitude, whereas most migrants travel twice yearly across a quarter of the globe. Their foraging routines should vary quite a bit between their tropical wintering grounds and the bleak Arctic coasts where they spend the brief northern summer. At both these extremes of habitat, I am sure there is still much to be discovered by observers with an open mind as well as a perceptive eye.

The most intensive research on falcons, wild as well as captive, has been centered on their reproduction and breeding. This is one important area where I know very little from first-hand experience, at least until quite recently. The reason is simple. A few years after I

178

moved to Alberta, the species all but disappeared as a breeding bird from much of the province. However, now more than three decades later, the peregrine's fortunes have been reversed and opportunities for nest-site observation abound. In Edmonton, the urban falcon population has grown to three or four pairs. However, cities are not an attractive environment for watching falcons, at least not for me. Instead, I have waited until the falcons made their triumphant return to their former haunts, the rivers. During the period when pairs were establishing territories in urban centers, I and others had occasionally checked cliffs in rural Alberta where peregrines had bred prior to the great decline. Near Edmonton, on the North Saskatchewan River, these searches have remained unproductive as of this writing. But the great day arrived in 1997 when Rob Corrigan discovered the first nests on natural sites on the Red Deer, as detailed in the chapter titled "Return to the River." The dynamics of this population will be followed closely in the coming years.

Unfortunately, the first pair I watched in the Valley of the Falcons failed to fledge young in their second season due to inclement weather. On June 27, 1998, a very wet and windy day, I saw the male retrieve a dead chick from below the nest ledge. He carried the carcass along for a while, winging slowly against the wind and doubling back several times, as if he were performing a sad ritual. He briefly landed on several spots before selecting a final resting place high on the cliff. Perhaps the dead chick was to be retrieved later and utilized as food? (Gordon Court assures me that incidents of cannibalism are not uncommon on the Arctic coast of Keewatin.) In the meantime, the remaining chick or chicks were brooded continuously by the female. I could see her head and part of her body as she crouched low among the waving nettles growing on the nest ledge which did not have a protected overhang and was quite exposed to the north wind. From time to time the female shook the moisture off her face. She obviously caught the brunt of the cold spell while temperatures dropped to two or three degrees above freezing. A few days later, I found that none of her precious progeny had survived.

However, on this same river, four other pairs successfully fledged a brood. Their future looks quite secure. These "manmade" falcons should continue to do well, paralleling the success of other populations recently recovering from their former troubles.

A peregrine is a peregrine is a peregrine

The peregrine's return to this central Alberta river, through the effort of human agencies, has delighted me perhaps more than most since I was there in the old days, and I am one of very few people who now actually spends time observing the new birds on the block. Just for the record and from a purely academic point of view, I am fascinated by more than just their ecology. In what respects are these newly colonizing falcons different from the ones that nested here formerly? Who can tell? Regretfully, no study skins collected prior to the 1970s seem to exist. During the time when the gradual process of extirpation was taking place, few took the trouble to look. I for one did, but all I have left are memories. They include vivid mental pictures of angry females swooping overhead on the few occasions that I actually approached too closely in an attempt to look into the nest from above. Cacking hoarsely, these falcons created a lasting impression of massive, awesome power. By comparison, and based on very few examples, I think that the new occupants of the Valley of the Falcons were not quite in the same weight class as their predecessors. The female of the pair observed in the summers of 1997 and 1998 was very slender. Even though her numbered leg band proved that she had been hatched and released in the summer of 1995, her dorsal plumage did not look adult. Back and wings were dark brown, blotched with a bit of gray, very unlike the great blue falcons that used to inhabit this valley. By contrast, her mate, although he looked smaller than a crow, was very handsome. His malar stripe was so wide as to practically form a black hood. Dorsally, his color showed a marked contrast between the pearl gray of the rump, the dark gray of the wings and the blackish tail. This striking dorsal pattern showed up best if the bird was in flight and seen in good light. Such variegated plumage was typical of falcons that I used to see each spring at Beaverhills Lake, prior to the mid-1970s. I considered it a diagnostic field mark of the big "duck hawks" that were first to arrive. They also hunted crows. I have not seen these massive *anatum* falcons in many years. And I have not seen attacks on crows for a very long time. Although relative size is a poor criterion in the field, I still encounter the odd falcon that looks as big as they come. However, the vast majority of migrants seem to be of medium size and very slender. Some are dorsally very dark, others light in color. The latter are probably typical of the tundra variety that nest in Arctic regions. The darker types, as mentioned in chapter one, may originate from the boreal forest regions of Canada. They should form an intermediate between *anatum* and *tundrius*. Of course, such a gradual intergradation or cline between the two subspecies, over a wide belt of continent, is only logical and to be expected.

Quite another question is this: if some of the reintroduced peregrines now nesting along the Red Deer River are indeed not as large as their predecessors, why should this be so? Is it a matter of genetics? To answer this question, we have to know the origin of the stock used in the breeding programs at Wainwright, where the present free-flying birds were produced. Some of the first captives included the last individuals nesting in central Alberta, rescued from oblivion by the program's originator, Richard Fyfe. However, other birds and eggs were obtained from the boreal regions far to the north, near Lake Athabasca and the Mackenzie River. In addition, the odd peregrine was added to the stable from Colorado. Interbreeding between them has therefore resulted in a progeny with bloodlines from a wide range of latitudes. This is no reason to consider these captive-raised birds in any way inferior. A peregrine is a peregrine is a peregrine. Similarly, the falcons that were reintroduced into the eastern United States by Dr. Tom Cade and his colleagues at The Peregrine Fund were the offspring of a mix of breeding stock from across the continent and even from Europe.

Only those people directly involved in the Alberta breeding program might be able to say whether or not there has been, over several generations of captive falcons, a selection favoring small over large or vice-versa. Which were the most productive? If there was a reduction in size over the long haul, was this perhaps a question of nutrition?

What are, possibly, the implications of size for the falcons that now have returned to the wilds of central Alberta? This is another fascinating question. It might not necessarily be a bad thing to be small, depending upon the kind of prey base available. The males of the eyries at Red Deer and Wabamun, while I watched, brought in only items the size of sparrows or shorebirds. Both tiercels obviously were excellent providers, catching enough prey to feed their mate and their young. It is a well-established fact that small passerines are also the mainstay of the tundra falcons that nest in Arctic regions and on Greenland.

Nothing is known about the diet of the peregrines that used to breed in central Alberta. The large females might have been dependent upon a good supply of medium-sized prey such as waterfowl, which are today less common on the plains due to changes in agricultural practices. Given the fact that the most numerous avian family is now blackbirds, a small peregrine might do better than a large duck hawk. As far as the male is concerned, his nearest competitor for food should be the merlin! However, on the breeding grounds along the Red Deer River, a more potent adversary remains the prairie falcon. Since this early-arriving and hardy raptor feeds its young mainly on ground squirrels, it does not compete with the peregrine for prey. However, nest site rivalry is quite another matter.

Peregrine versus prairie falcon

The last of my speculative questions is this: would body size make a difference in the vicious battle between peregrines and prairies? Would a big falcon be better than a small one at driving off the opponent? Can a pair of peregrines actually take a nest site away from a pair of prairie falcons, as some observers have reported elsewhere? On the Red Deer River, as of 1998 after two breeding seasons, the jury is still out on this fascinating issue. At one site in the valley, a pair of peregrines, vastly superior in the skies, appeared to share a small but prominent cliff with a pair of prairie falcons. Later in the season, Rob Corrigan found that the latter had managed to raise their three young successfully despite the presence of their aggressive cousins. Even more puzzling was the fact that the peregrine male was seen to bring food to the prairie falcon chicks!

The background of this confusing situation is unclear. A scrape on the edge of the same cliff seemed to indicate the peregrines may indeed have attempted to start their own family. However, the ledge was easily accessible to humans as well as four-footed predators. The scrape, near the top of the cliff, was examined by Gordon Court, who picked up a peregrine feather as well as the scat of a coyote from the spot! The prairie falcon nest, by contrast, was in a well-sheltered cave, less than forty yards (35 m) away.

At the other four peregrine nesting cliffs on the Red Deer, inter-specific strife was avoided since prairie falcons were absent. Three of these sites were former hack locations, where captive-raised pere-grines had been released from 1992 until 1995. The fourth site was the eyrie I watched in 1997 and 1998. Here, in a one-mile (1.6 km) section of the Valley of the Falcons, on the same side of the river, there were two successful eyries of prairie falcons and one of pere-grines, as well as the roost of a lone prairie. This illustrates that there is, in fact, a great deal of tolerance between the two species of fal-cons, as long as they do not set their sights on the same spot! Incidentally, both prairie falcon eyries were on traditional sites where I had found the species nesting during the 1960s. Moreover, as reported in chapter four, the peregrines had chosen the exact same cliff as their predecessors thirty years earlier! There was one major difference between the eyries. Those of the two pairs of prairie falcons featured a well-protected ledge complete with overhang. By contrast, as mentioned earlier, the peregrines had chosen an open ledge exposed to the elements, with tragic consequences for their brood.

To this date, available evidence tends to indicate the latter have to make do with sites not traditionally held by prairie falcons. However, once the boundaries between the two species have been determined, there appears to be little friction between them. This was exactly the same conclusion I had reached in the 1960s. However, this notion is not cast in stone. The opposite may happen in future, especially if the peregrines should expand their population with vigor. The next few years will provide a sequel to this intrigu-ing saga, the return of the native and its ancient rivalry with the other grand master of the prairie skies.

Appendix

Prey species seen to be captured by peregrines at various localities. List updated to September 1998. Not included are remains of prey found in the field, even if peregrines were seen to be feeding on them.

BL=Beaverhills Lake, AB
VI=Vancouver Island, BC
QC=Queen Charlotte Islands, BC

BB=Boundary Bay, BC
PP=Powerplant, AB
EW=elsewhere

	BL	VI	QC	BB	PP	EW
Small Grebe (Unidentified)	1	–	–	–	–	–
Green-winged Teal	5	5	–	–	–	–
Mallard	2	–	–	–	–	–
Northern Pintail	6	13	–	1	–	–
Blue-winged Teal	1	–	–	–	–	–
Northern Shoveler	5	–	–	–	–	–
Gadwall	3	–	–	–	–	–
American Wigeon	1	17	–	–	–	–
Eurasian Wigeon	–	–	–	–	–	1
Ring-necked Duck	–	1	–	–	–	–
Lesser Scaup	5	–	–	–	–	–
Bufflehead	–	–	–	–	1	–
American Coot	1	–	–	–	–	–
Ducks (Unidentified)	4	6	–	–	1	–
Black-bellied Plover	2	–	–	–	–	–
American Golden Plover	1	–	–	–	–	–
Lesser Yellowlegs	4	–	–	–	–	–
Sanderling	1	–	–	–	–	–
Semipalmated Sandpiper	4	–	–	–	–	–
Least Sandpiper	2	–	–	–	–	–
Baird's Sandpiper	3	–	–	–	–	–
Pectoral Sandpiper	22	–	–	–	–	–
Dunlin	–	–	–	28	–	–
Stilt Sandpiper	1	–	–	–	–	–
Buff-breasted Sandpiper	1	–	–	–	–	–
Sandpiper (Unidentified)	13	–	–	–	–	–
Dowitcher	2	–	–	–	–	–
Wilson's Phalarope	1	–	–	–	–	–
Phalarope (Unidentified)	–	–	2	–	–	–
Shorebird (Unidentified)	6	–	–	–	3	–
Franklin's Gull	2	–	–	–	2	–
Common Tern	1	–	–	–	–	–
Murrelets and Auklets	–	–	13	–	–	–
Sea birds (Unidentified)	–	–	1	–	–	–
Rock Dove	–	2	–	–	–	1
Common Nighthawk	–	–	–	–	–	2
American Robin	–	3	–	–	–	–
Savannah Sparrow	1	–	–	–	–	–
Snow Bunting	2	–	–	–	–	–
Passerines (Unidentified)	–	–	–	–	14	–
Birds (Unidentified)	–	–	–	–	2	–
TOTALS (222)	**103**	**47**	**16**	**29**	**23**	**4**

Hunting success rates of peregrines recorded by the author at various localities.

Number of hunts	Prey species	Number of captures	Percent success	Locality* (Season)	Year of** publication
569	Shorebirds	50	8.8	BL (Migration)	1988
302	Shorebirds	28	9.3	BB (Winter)	1998
275	Ducks	25	9.3	BL (Migration)	1987
43	Ducks	09	20.9	VI (Winter)	1987
73	Seabirds	16	21.9	QC (Summer)	1997
108	various	23	21.3	PP (Summer)	1999***

* For location codes, see page 184.

** For publications of the author, see References. (After these papers were published more data have been collected in various study areas but have not yet been tabulated.)

*** See Chapter 14.

Note: The last three entries pertain to adult peregrines on territory, either in winter or summer.

References

The peregrine is a very well-researched species. The list of scientific papers, books, theses and unpublished reports, now at about two thousand, is still growing. The following are publications by the author and others that contain information of relevance for this book.

Anderson, C. M. and P. D. DeBruyn. 1979. *Behavior and ecology of peregrine falcons wintering on the Skagit Flats, Washington State*. Unpublished Report. Department of Game, Olympia, WA. 53 pp.

Baker, J. A. 1967. *The peregrine*. Collins, London, U. K. 191 pp.

Beebe, F. L. 1960. "The marine peregrines of the northwest Pacific coast." *Condor* 62:145-189.

Bent, A. C. 1938. (Dover reprint 1961). *Life histories of North American birds of prey*. Part 2. Smithsonian Institution, New York. 482 pp.

Bird, D. M. and Y. Aubry. 1982. "Reproductive and hunting behavior in peregrine falcons, *Falco peregrinus*, in southern Quebec." *Canadian Field-Naturalist* 96:167-171.

Bradley, D. M. and L. W. Oliphant. 1991. "The diet of peregrine falcons in Rankin Inlet, Northwest Territories: an unusually high proportion of mammalian prey." *Condor* 93:193-197.

Brown, L. and D. Amadon. 1968. *Eagles, hawks and falcons of the world*. Hamlyn House, Feltham, U. K. 945 pp.

Buchanan, J. B. 1996. "A comparison of behavior and success rates of merlins and peregrine falcons when hunting dunlins in two coastal habitats." *Journal of Raptor Research* 30:93-98.

Burnham, B. 1997. *A fascination with falcons*. Hancock House Publishers, Surrey, British Columbia. 233 pp.

Butler, R. W. 1994. Distribution and abundance of western sandpipers, dunlins, and black-bellied plovers in the Fraser Estuary. Pages 18-23 in: *The abundance and distribution of estuarine birds in the Strait of Georgia, British Columbia*. Edited by R. W. Butler and K. Vermeer. Canadian Wildlife Service Occasional Paper No. 83, Ottawa. 79 pp.

Cade, T. J. 1982. *The falcons of the world*. Cornell University Press, Ithaca, N. Y. 192 pp.

Cade, T. J., J. H. Enderson, C. G. Thelander, and C. M. White, (Editors). 1988. *Peregrine falcon populations: their management and recovery*. The Peregrine Fund, Boise, Idaho. 949 pp.

Cochran, W. W. 1985. *Ocean migration of peregrine falcons: is the adult male pelagic?* Pages 223-237 in: Proceedings of Hawk Migration Conference IV. M. Harwood, Editor. Hawk Migration Association of North America.

Court, G. S. 1986. Some aspects of the reproductive biology of tundra peregrine falcons. M. Sc. thesis, University of Alberta, Edmonton, Canada. 121 pp.

Court, G. S. , C. C. Gates, and D. A. Boag. 1988. "Natural history of the peregrine falcon in the Keewatin District of the Northwest Territories." *Arctic* 41:17-30.

Court, G. S. 1993. *A toxicological assessment of the American peregrine falcon breeding in Alberta, Canada, 1968 to 1992.* Alberta Fish and Wildlife Services, Wildlife Management Divison. Occasional Paper 10.

Court, G. S. , S. Brechtel, G. Erickson, and B. Treichel. 1996. *The future of the peregrine falcon (Falco peregrinus anatum) in Alberta.* Proceedings of the 4th annual prairie endangered species conference. Lethbridge, Alberta, 1995.

Cresswell, W. 1996. "Surprise as a winter hunting strategy in sparrowhawks, *Accipiter nisus*, peregrines, *Falco peregrinus*, and merlins, *Falco columbarius.*" *Ibis* 138:684-692.

Dekker, D. 1967. "Disappearance of the peregrine falcon as a breeding bird in a river valley in Alberta." *Blue Jay* 30:175-176.

———. 1979. "Characteristics of peregrine falcons migrating through central Alberta, 1969-1978." *Canadian Field-Naturalist* 93:296-302.

———. 1980. "Hunting success rates, foraging habits, and prey selection of peregrine falcons migrating through central Alberta." *Canadian Field-Naturalist* 94:371-382.

———. 1984. "Spring and fall migrations of peregrine falcons in central Alberta, 1979-1983, with comparisons to 1969-1978." *Raptor Research* 18:92-97.

———. 1985. *Wild hunters - Adventures with wolves, foxes, eagles and falcons based on 25 years of field observation.* Canadian Wolf Defenders Publication, Edmonton. 224 pp.

———. 1987. "Peregrine falcon predation on ducks in Alberta and British Columbia." *Journal of Wildlife Management* 51:156-159.

———. 1988. "Peregrine falcon and merlin predation on small shorebirds and passerines in Alberta." *Canadian Journal of Zoology* 66:925-928.

———. 1991 (1998). *Prairie water. Wildlife at Beaverhills Lake, Alberta.* University of Alberta Press, Edmonton. 148 pp.

———. 1993. "Valley of the falcons." *Alberta Naturalist* 23(3):53-56.

———. 1995. "Prey capture by peregrine falcons wintering on southern Vancouver Island, British Columbia." *Journal of Raptor Research* 29:26-29.

———. 1996. *Hawks - Hunters on the wing.* NorthWord Wildlife Series. NorthWord Press, Wisconsin. 144 pp.

———. and L. Bogaert. 1997. "Over-ocean hunting by peregrine falcons in British Columbia." *Journal of Raptor Research* 31:381-383.

———. 1998. "Over-ocean flocking by dunlins, *Calidris alpina*, and the effect of predation at Boundary Bay, British Columbia." *Canadian Field-Naturalist* 112 (4).

Enderson, J. H. , W. Heinrich, L. Kiff, and C. M. White. 1995. *Population changes in North American peregrines.* Pages 142-161 in: Transactions of the 60th North American Wildlife and Natural Resources Conference.

Enderson, J. H. and G. R. Craig. 1997. "Wide ranging by nesting peregrine falcons as determined by radiotelemetry." *Journal of Raptor Research* 31:333-338.

Eutermoser, A. 1961. "Schlagen Beizfalken bevorzugt kranke Krähen?" *Vogelwelt* 82:101-104.

Frank, S. 1994. *City peregrines. A ten-year saga of New York City falcons.* Hancock House Publishers. 313 pp.

Fyfe, R. W. 1976. "Rationale and success of the Canadian Wildlife Service peregrine breeding project." *Canadian Field-Naturalist* 90:308-319.

Hickey, J. J. 1969. (Editor). *Peregrine falcon populations: their biology and decline.* University of Wisconsin Press, Madison. 596 pp.

Holroyd, G. L. and U. Banasch. 1990. "The reintroduction of the peregrine falcon, *Falco peregrinus anatum*, into southern Canada." *Canadian Field-Naturalist* 104:203-208.

Hunt, W. G. , R. R. Rogers and D. J. Slowe. 1975. "Migratory and foraging behavior of peregrine falcons on the Texas coast." *Canadian Field-Naturalist* 89:111-123.

Johnstone, R. M., G. S. Court, A. C. Fesser, D. M. Bradley, L. W. Oliphant, and J. D. MacNeil. 1996. "Long-term trends and sources of organochlorine contamination in Canadian tundra peregrine falcons." *Environmental Pollution* 93:109-120.

Nelson, R. W. 1970. Some aspects of the breeding behavior of peregrine falcons on Langara Island, British Columbia. M. Sc. thesis, University of Calgary, Alberta. 306 pp.

————. 1990. "Status of the peregrine falcon, *Falco peregrinus pealei*, on Langara Island, Queen Charlotte Islands, British Columbia, 1968-1989." *Canadian Field-Naturalist* 104:193-199.

Page, G. and D. F. Whitacre. 1975. "Raptor predation on wintering shorebirds." *Condor* 77:73- 83.

Palmer, R. S. 1988. *Handbook of North American birds.* Volume 5, diurnal raptors, part 2. Yale Univ. Press, New Haven. 465 pp.

Parker, A. 1979. "Peregrines at a Welsh coastal eyrie." *British Birds* 72:104æ–114.

Piersma, T. 1994. Close to the edge: Energetic bottlenecks and the evolution of migratory pathways in knots. Ph. D. Thesis. Rijksuniversiteit Groningen, The Netherlands. 366 pp.

Ratcliffe, D. 1993. *The peregrine falcon.* Academic Press, San Diego, CA. 454 pp.

Roalkvam, R. 1985. "How effective are hunting peregrines?" *Raptor Research* 19:27-29.

Rose, B. J. 1965. "Notes on a peregrine falcon and Franklin's gull encounter." *Blue Jay* 28:163.

Rudebeck, G. 1950-1951. "The choice of prey and modes of hunting of predatory birds with special reference to their selective effect." *Oikos* 2: 67-88, 3:200-231.

Sherrod, S. 1983. *Post-fledging behavior of the peregrine falcon.* The Peregrine Fund, Ithaca, New York. 202 pp.

Swanston, R. 1998. "Peregrine falcons hunting over greenhouse light." *Discovery.* Vancouver Natural History Society, B.C.

Tatum, J. B. 1981. "Peregrine fishing at sea." *British Birds* 74:97.

Treleaven, R. B. 1977. *The private life of the peregrine.* Headland Publications, Penzance, G. B. 152 pp.

————. 1980. "High and low intensity hunting in raptors." *Zeitschrift für Tierpsychologie* 54:339-345.

————. 1981. "Peregrine feeding herring gull chick to young." *British Birds* 74:97.

Voous, K. H. 1961. "Records of peregrine falcons on the Atlantic Ocean." *Ardea* 49:176-177.

White, C. M. 1968. "Diagnosis and relationships of the North American tundra-inhabiting peregrine falcons." *Auk* 85: 179-191.

Index